I0485607

PRINCIPLES OF BUSINESS
For The Caribbean

Rawle Cyprian Eastmond JP BA Dip Ed LLB LEC LLM
Wendell C C Callender JP BA DipEd BSc

©

All rights reserved. No part of this publication may be reproduced, stored in retrieval system, or transmitted, in any form or by any means, electronic, mechanical, photocopying, recording or otherwise, without the prior permission of the Publishers.

Published 2016

ISBN-10: 1517415047
ISBN-13: 978-1517415044

Published by

Wencal Media

'Charleston', Government Hill, St. Michael, Barbados, West Indies

Tel (246) 571-8715; (246) 255-0993

 Email: wendellcallender@msn.com

Cover Design by

MDC Office Services,

'Silver Sands, Christ Church, Barbados, West Indies.

Tel (246) 428-2797; (246) 249-7025

E-mail: m.callender@live.com

FOREWORD

This book has been written for all persons interested in how business is conducted within the Caribbean. However the writers have given great consideration to providing a practical text for students who are pursuing Principles of Business at the Caribbean Examinations Council's CSEC Level.

The writers of this publication have both been teachers of Principles of Business at this level for a combined total of forty years and have been practitioners in several fields of business in the Caribbean. They bring practical insights to the study of business and are also mindful of the challenges which students face in grappling with this subject.

Each chapter has a number of Research topics which encourages the students to pursue further individual research. The questions at the end of the Chapters also provide scope for the students to focus on key topics presented in the Chapters and should be useful revision tools.

A Multiple-Choice Test also assists as a revision guide.

Principles of Business for the Caribbean brings the study of business alive!

CONTENTS

	Chapter	Page
1.	Early economies	5
2.	First principles of economics	14
3.	Getting started in business	21
4.	Nature of business	27
5.	Types of business units	31
6.	Production	36
7.	Internal organisational environment	46
8.	Marketing	57
9.	Distribution and selling	69
10.	Human resource management	75
11.	Sources of finance	81
12.	Business accounting	84
13.	Market structures and price determination	95
14.	Everyday factors which influence customer behavior	102
15.	Consumer protection	109
16.	Money, banking and finance	116
17.	Insurance	125
18.	Business documents	132
19.	Legal aspects of business	139
20.	Government	148
21.	Social accounting	154
22.	CARICOM and CSME	163
23.	Regional and global business environment	174
24.	Economic problems in the Caribbean	179
25.	Multiple choice questions	188
26.	Answers to multiple choice questions	200
27.	About the authors	201

CHAPTER 1

EARLY ECONOMIES

In many parts of the world there were economies that can best be described as Stone-Age type economies. These economies showed that way back in time, early man was a hunter. He became a farmer afterwards.

Improvements in the well-being of humankind came when early people learnt how to plant food crops and rear and reap them.

In the Stone Age, tools were made of stone and put to use. Stone tools were used to help prepare the ground for the planting of crops and for other purposes as well. Bows and arrows were also used by Stone Age people.

There is evidence that even though in olden days some people lived in caves, by the time they learnt to make materials like the wood they got from the limbs and branches of different trees, they could choose to live outside of caves.

In the Stone Age, too, people discovered fire which would have been used to clear the land, provide heat for them in their houses and also for the preparation and cooking of their meals. One of the characteristics of the earliest economies was that these economies depended almost exclusively on agriculture and fishing.

However before commercial agriculture was developed in earliest times, each family and household set out to provide for its own livelihood. Before people learnt how to plant seeds, make fire and carve and make stone tools, their food supply was very uncertain and in cases where they hunted animals for food, no doubt using strong sticks and clubs, they ran the risk of being attacked by the larger animals. When circumstances improved and early people found ways of better manipulating their environment, they became able to better meet mankind's basic needs which are:

- Food
- Clothing
- Shelter

To this day these three remain the basic needs of humankind and in the olden days would have been met with considerable effort, largely through direct production.

DIRECT PRODUCTION

When people produce all of their own goods themselves, production is said to be direct. It can be said that under a system of direct production, producer and consumer are one and the same person. It is different with indirect production.

INDIRECT PRODUCTION

This may be defined as a system of production where persons make use of goods which they do not produce for themselves only, but are made available by others. Implied in a system of indirect production is that there exists a body of specialist producers who make goods and services available to the market.

EARLY TRADE

Trade can be defined as the sale and exchange of goods and services.

It has always been accepted that trade becomes possible when the seller is in possession of surplus goods and services or is in a position to make things available for sale to third parties.

In some very early economies there were persons who ended up producing more goods than they needed for themselves. Where people's production exceeds their own personal needs it is normal to speak of surplus production. Surplus production makes it possible to sell and trade.

In today's world where indirect production leads to trade, many goods are sold in large quantities and in many cases far away from where they were produced. Money is used both in local trade and international trade.

However years ago before the days of ocean going ships and aircraft, trade was conducted within limited borders.

Of note too early trade was conducted by means of barter.

BARTER

Barter is the swapping or exchange of goods for goods. Money is not used for the purchase of goods.

In simple economies people used barter as the means of trade but it presented problems.

Consider the (2) scenarios below:

Toto has yams for sale and wants eddoes in exchange. He meets eight people over a twelve mile stretch all of whom want to 'buy' yams but who have no eddoes. Toto returns home with his yams having never got any eddoes.

Victory wants avocados and has sweet potatoes for 'sale'. She spent twelve hours searching for persons who had avocados available and meets Tim who does have avocados and lucky for Victory, Tim wishes to buy sweet potatoes.

So Tim has what Victory wants and Victory has what Tim wants. To this extent there could be trade but a problem exists. Victory argues that her sweet potatoes are of greater value than Tim's avocadoes.

Barter can only occur where there is a double coincidence of wants and things like value are agreed.

Problems with Barter

1. It is often hard to find the perfect trading partner. The seller's true trading partner may be miles away.
2. It wastes time and it also causes long hard searches.
3. There may be issues with value and even weight and quality as well.

Does Barter have a positive side?

Some modern countries either on account of diplomatic relations and friendships or because of foreign exchange difficulties, barter with others. Dominica has been known to sell soap to Guyana in exchange for rice.

MONEY

Money can be described as:

(a) A medium of exchange.
(b) A unit of measurement.
(c) A store of value
(d) A unit of account.

Money facilitates exchange while putting measurable values on items. Money itself when stored always has a value.

Legal Tender

Nowadays in nearly every part of the world money consists either of currency made from special paper or of coins. In olden days things like cowrite shells, beads, pieces of metal, animals such as goats, and many other things were used as money.

In today's modern world coins are used in everyday business transactions but are never marked 'legal tender'. Strictly speaking coins are not fully 'legal tender'. They are not legal tender for the payment of any amount.

However local bank notes such as $5.00, $10.00, $50.00 and $100.00 and many foreign bank notes clearly state that they are legal tender for the payment of any amount.

What this means is that when bank notes are presented as payment, they must be accepted.

THE QUALITY OF LIFE OF THE EARLY PEOPLE

People who lived in Stone Age economies did not have wheeled vehicles, electricity, piped water or telephones.

Indeed they would not have had radios, television sets or computers.

In early Stone Age cultures there were no public social services such as those made available in today's modern hospitals, schools and health clinics.

Some Stone Age people continued to live in cold caves even after fire was discovered and houses were built by some others.

Finding proper medicines would have been most challenging for the early people.

It is certain that in the Stone Age life expectancy was low and where trade by barter was cumbersome and inconvenient many people would not have found it easy to secure what they wanted.

The standard of living of a people refers to the quality of life people enjoy. Persons who barely eke out an existence and have just the basics of life do not enjoy a good quality life, while those who have access to luxuries and comforts will enjoy a better life and greater satisfaction.

'Standard of living' which must never be confused with 'cost of living' clearly refers to the wellbeing of a people.

In instances where people only have access to basic food (starchy food) and a little more, and to poor housing and cheap clothes only, even though these people are making ends meet, their quality of life and well-being would be quite low and poor. Others who have the means to consume expensive luxurious clothes, fine houses, expensive rich flavoured foods along with many other amenities and luxuries will experience a higher standard of living.

Finally people make use of goods and services for the satisfaction which these things provide. Economists refer to this satisfaction as utility.

Economists when they consider that some people use very, very expensive goods, cigarettes, cigars and such like do not impose value judgments on the motive(s) why some people use things which are avoided by others.

Today's modern economy is a far cry from that of the economy of the Stone Age because today's people live in a world with thousands of goods and services which were neither available to nor known by the early people.

NATURE OF PRODUCTION

In considering the nature of production it is necessary to look at the type, character and state of what is being or has been produced. Production tends to be of three types: Primary, Secondary and Tertiary.

Primary Production

As its name suggests this category of production refers to goods at the very first stage of production.

Practical experience shows that quarrying and mining materials straight from the earth or sea in an unrefined state is the first stage or extractive primary stage of production.

Similarly, unrefined and unprocessed agricultural commodities extracted from the earth in their natural state are examples of goods produced at the primary level of production.

Finally, it is obvious that extractive production derives from Mother Nature and so any product which clearly originates from the natural environment which did not undergo transformation or treatment leading to refinement is and will be primary production.

It follows therefore that if Mr. Chanderpaul grows vegetables he would be involved in primary production. Of note, livestock and poultry are considered to be 'goods' at the primary level of production.

Secondary Production

Raw goods are often made to undergo some change. Where items like carrots, peas, beans, fish and other raw products are made to undergo some processing or change character from their natural state to a more refined or processed state, a higher form of production comes into issue. This is referred to as secondary production.

The manufacture of sweets and beer also takes place at the secondary stage of production. One of the characteristics of manufacturing as far as agro processing is concerned is that the secondary production and transformation of agricultural goods does provide for the preservation of goods which would otherwise have perished.

Tertiary Production

In all Caribbean countries commercial banks, insurance companies and hotels exist. These institutions provide services to their customers/clients. These are considered tertiary production.

Other services which are part of tertiary production include education, health, transport, financial services, shipping, banking and similar services which facilitate the conduct of business.

A service tends to be 'invisible' compared with a tangible item like a good or commodity which is visible.

There now follows discussion on Levels or Amounts of Production.

The Levels of Production are

- Subsistence
- Domestic
- Export

A.   SUBSISTENCE

If the total amount of products or services produced is below commercial quantities and is not seen or required to attract cash purchases the level of production is said to be subsistence.

If Mr. Clive Garcia of Near Rio Hondo, Belize grows just enough carrots for his family and to give his neighbours freely, he could be said to be engaged in subsistence farming.

Subsistence production has for years been seen by many to involve the production of goods but it is possible for people to perform subsistence-type services.

Consider a young lady called Gaitre Muhammed who practices her skill as a hairdresser for her family and friends without fee or charge. Hairdressing is a service and in this example Gaitre is not selling her services as a hairdresser for commercial purposes or in commercial quantities.

B.   DOMESTIC PRODUCTION

Goods and services produced in amounts which exceed the wants of their producers and which are not for export but are to be sold and consumed locally could be said to be produced either for the domestic market only, or at the domestic level of production.

So if St. Lucia does not export any of its carrots and yams but consumes them locally, quantities consistent with the domestic level have been produced.

In many ways if any country is entirely self-sufficient in crops and commodities AND DOES NOT EXPORT, domestic production occurs.

As Caribbean countries move completely into free trade both within the CSME and the WTO they will find that they cannot easily refuse products similar to their own from entering into their markets. This matter will raise many issues some of which will be dealt with elsewhere in this book.

C.   EXPORTING GOODS AND SERVICES

Years ago when a country exported it meant that it had produced a surplus such that it had enough to meet domestic demand with some production left over.

However on occasions a country may without selling a given good in its own market make it available for export.

In the 1990s Barbados sold all its sugar to the E.U. in exchange for foreign exchange, and imported sugar from Guyana after earlier having bought this commodity from Guatemala.

There are North American businesses that have set up in the Caribbean to sell their products to third world countries.

Increasingly in recent years, institutions offering special services like insurance and banking have been established in the Caribbean under particular tax treaties and incentives.
These institutions are located in various Caribbean countries but their owners and investors live abroad. They are referred to as offshore businesses and they export services abroad.

Where a Caribbean country exports goods and services abroad it earns foreign exchange. Trade in goods is called visible trade while the export and import of services are called invisible trade. Both visible and invisible trade carries implications for foreign exchange transactions.

A BRIEF WORD ABOUT NATIONAL SPECIALIZATION

For purposes of this section 'specialization' will not be used in the sense as the division of labour but instead refers to instances where a nation or country concentrates almost exclusively on a single crop or single sector.

MONOCULTURE

When a country produces just one crop as its sole cash crop it is specialising in the production of just one commodity.

Caribbean economies have up to relatively recently experienced monoculture e.g. bananas in St. Vincent, Dominica, St. Lucia.

What explains Monoculture?

1. In the colonial days the 'mother country' set up economies which depended on but one crop.
2. Where conditions like terrain, soil types and the availability of cheap labour proved helpful to and supportive of the one crop, local producers would produce it.
3. Where a given country became renowned for the one crop and its by-products it was said to have a comparative advantage meaning that compared with other products from other countries it held an edge over others e.g. The Sugar, Molasses and Rum of Barbados before the Barbadian economy underwent diversification.

Disadvantages of Monoculture

1. Its excessive dependence on one commodity means that if that commodity experienced downturn or decline, its country will lose a substantial amount of earnings.
2. An economy built on but one commodity is built on an unsafe foundation.
3. Where other countries (competitors) produce the identical commodity at lower prices, business will be lost to the country in question.
4. Where the population of a given country is extremely large it is unthinkable that all persons will be employed in the production of this solitary commodity.
5. If overseas buyers stop purchasing the commodity it may be difficult to find new trading parties in the short-term.
6. If overseas importers reduce the price, earnings fall e.g. Bananas from Dominica, Bananas from St. Vincent, Sugar from Barbados.
7. Where earnings from Caribbean exports fall, local producers will respond by attempting to cut costs and in many cases cost cutting means retrenching workers.
8. All in all, even when a country has earned a reputation as being extremely competent in pushing a particular commodity – asserting that it has a clear comparative advantage – it is very, very risky to structure an entire economy on but one sector.

RESEARCH TASKS

1. Was there ever a Stone Age in the Caribbean?
2. Present proof that years ago there might have been people who practiced Stone Age type economic activity.
3. What facilitates indirect production and what are the characteristics of this type of production?
4. Outline the problems associated with barter.
5. Find out what gives rise to trade.

QUESTIONS

1. Outline the day-to-day activities of Stone Age people.
2. Comment on the challenges faced by Stone Age people in maintaining a livelihood.
3. Provide two examples of Stone Age tools.
4. How true would it be to state that tertiary production was unknown to Stone Age people?

CHAPTER 2

FIRST PRINCIPLES IN ECONOMICS: AN INTRODUCTION

The word 'economy' may be defined as the system by which the total resources of a country blend together or are brought together in a way that leads to the production and availability of goods and services for use by persons who are affected by the economy with which they have a relationship.

This is one possible definition of the term 'economy' but in the real world it is often easier to describe aspects of an economy and to point to things that relate to the economy without finding it easy to define economy in precise or concise terms.

The term 'economy' is a complex one.

CONSTITUENT PARTS OF AN ECONOMY

The total natural resources of a country including:

1. The oceans, beaches and seas.
2. Those plants that grow out of the land.
3. Special products that come from the land and sea, e.g. marl, limestone from quarries, raw red mud good for bauxite, oil from under the sea.
4. A country's human resources.
5. The local currency of the country which is in circulation in the retail banking sector and held by merchants and consumers.
6. The foreign reserves of a given country.
7. The sun for solar power.
8. The wind for energy driven by the wind.

WHAT IS ECONOMICS

To many persons economics is the study of the allocation of scarce resources. This is a general description of the science of economics but another possible definition is:

"the science that reveals what is available to a country and its people, …. and how people go about planning their livelihoods as they seek to make a living and the things that affect a person's and nation's livelihood."

This is a possible definition but it really is fairly difficult to define economics in an easy or precise manner. In practice there are institutions which have an influence on economics and the economy.

WHY ARE RESOURCES DEEMED SCARCE?

There are those whose opinion is that human wants are unlimited. Pursuing the argument that each person has unlimited desires but cannot possibly have what it takes to get everything on earth – and in the sky - the conclusion is reached that individuals then have to trim their wants and limit them simply because they are unable to fulfil their hopes and dreams to get everything.

IMPORTANT INSTITUTIONS IN CARIBBEAN ECONOMIES

One of the characteristics of all economies, including Caribbean economies, is that as production and consumption occur there are institutions which are established that in one way or another affect economic activity. Consider the part played by each of the following:

1. The Central Bank.
2. The Treasury and Inland Revenue.
3. Sea Port(s).
4. The Airport.
5. Farmers.
6. Public Transport Services.
7. Hospitals.
8. Different companies producing and selling many things at the level of manufacturing, wholesaling and retailing.
9. Unincorporated firms like Sole Proprietors and Partnerships in the Private Sector providing goods.
10. Law Firms.
11. Accounting Firms.
12. Construction Companies.
13. The Army and Defence Force.
14. The Police.
15. Public Housing Associations and Corporations.
16. Schools and Educational Institutions.

DETERMINING HOW INSTITUTIONS AFFECT ECONOMIC ACTIVITY

The Central Bank can increase interest rates making borrowing more costly. If they reduce these interest rates borrowing becomes cheaper. Similarly, Government can make changes to taxation.

Sea Ports and Airports can facilitate the export and import of goods and the movement of people. Law Firms and Accounting Firms can assist with the formation of businesses and in the case of accounting firms with financial advice.

The Police, Army and Fire Service which exist to protect and serve can make the business environment safe while schools and hospitals could position workers to be in a proper condition to be productive in their work places.

In addition the services offered by Banks and Insurance Companies can facilitate and protect various businesses.

DESCRIBING DIFFERENT ECONOMIES

Modern economies are considered to be either
  (1) Free Enterprise economies (Private Enterprise and Capitalism).
  (2) Centrally Planned economies or Collectivist Economies
  (3) Mixed Economies.

FREE ENTERPRISE ECONOMIES

The free or private enterprise type of economy is one which permits businesses to be owned by private individuals. It can be said therefore that individuals functioning outside of the state are free to own, manage and control their own businesses. Government is not involved in the ownership of these businesses which are set up primarily to earn profits for their owners and shareholders.

Where Government may get involved in the affairs of these private sector businesses it is for the purpose of taxing them, passing rules to ensure that they do not abuse their customers and insisting on things like proper health and safety practices. Otherwise, Government does not exert any influence on privately owned businesses which are free to determine such matters as system of management, size of management, size of workforce, which business institutions to deal with at the level of banks, insurance companies etc.

'Free Enterprise' contributes through employment, innovation, production of goods and services and payment of taxes to Government.

Advantages of the Free Enterprise system

1. Businesses are relatively free of Government control.
2. Businesses are free to decide exactly what products or services they should produce.
3. Where there are many private businesses, some of which produce identical products as other businesses functioning in the same economy, competition exists and the results of competition can mean
    (a) The consumers in the economy have a wider range of choice.
    (b) Businesses seek to outdo each other and in the process the consumer has available to them better quality.
    (c) Competition also leads to lower prices.
4. Successful private owned businesses could inspire new entrants to come into the market.

The Free Enterprise Sector is associated with democratic systems and cultures

Disadvantages of the Free Enterprise Economy:

1.   Some businesses profiteer and practice price gouging.
2.   Large businesses out-compete smaller ones since the larger businesses can benefit from -
        (a) Economies of Scale.
        (b) Economies of Scope, earning savings and reducing cost per unit.
        (c) Trade discounts.
        (d) Cash Discounts.
3.   In free enterprise systems many producers all together produce too much of the same product. To the extent that there would be dozens of different types of toilet paper and paper towels and two to twelve radio stations but not enough food and fruit nor farmers nor manufacturers a pertinent question is "From a social standpoint is some investment misallocated?"
4.   The free enterprise system tends to encourage excessive consumerism and wastage. The best example of a free enterprise economy is that of the United States of America.

THE CENTRALLY PLANNED OR COLLECTIVIST ECONOMY

This is an economy which is managed and controlled by the State. Under a centrally planned economy Government and the State control the commanding heights of the economy.

Advantages

1. Government can control the economy on behalf of and in favour of the population.
2. It will not be easy in a planned economy for some persons to be richer than others. Goods are allocated more fairly than under the free enterprise system.
3. Profiteering is non-existent under a Planned Economy.
4. The worst features and consequences of consumerism are avoided.
5. From a social standpoint there is balanced investment. A sensibly run collectivist economy will hardly allow fifteen to twenty different brands of toilet paper and twelve radio stations while there are insufficient farms and manufacturing industries.

Producers and Consumers are encouraged to bear the interests of society as a whole in mind and to refrain from being selfish.

Disadvantages

1. Centrally planned or collectivist economies tend to have huge bureaucracies leading to slowness in decision making, delay and inefficiencies.
2. Practical experience has shown that in centrally planned economies productivity among workers is low.

3. On account of an absence of competition, goods tend to be of a low quality.
4. There is significant product homogeneity.   In the absence of private sector involvement the state tends to produce goods that lack variety in character, quality and appeal.
5. Goods produced by state-run companies tend to be inefficiently produced.
6. The structure and character of centrally planned economies provide little or no reward for creativity, initiative and innovation and the result is that many talented persons who live in these economies do not feel encouraged to invent and innovate.
7. Centrally planned economies are noted for high levels of economic and political dictatorship which impact negatively on economic activity.

THE MIXED ECONOMY

A mixed economy presents some of the features of the capitalist or private enterprise economy and some of the features of a planned economy. Note how Government controls

     (i)   Armies
     (ii)   Police Forces
     (iii)   Fire Services
     (iv)   The provision of water.
     (v)   Public Hospitals and Clinics.
     (vi)   Other institutions which the private sector would consider as being absolutely unprofitable.

However Caribbean Governments have been known to participate in

     (vii)   Electricity Plants
     (vii)   Public schools, Colleges and Polytechnics.
     (viii)   Relatively cheap public transport.

But also note that as a general rule Governments in the Caribbean do not sell
     Clothes
     Timber
     Food

In the last thirty years some Caribbean Governments have owned commercial banks and insurance companies but in recent years these very banks and insurance companies have been privatized.

Some persons in the Caribbean feel that some private businesses should be nationalized and put under state control to prevent them from exploiting the public.

However in recent years there have been no strong proposals from Governments to take control of businesses which for years have been part of the private enterprise economy.

The mixed economy can bring together the best and most positive features of the free enterprise and planned economies and so the advantage of a mixed economy would be those better parts of both the free enterprise economy and the planned economic system and the negative in each of the two systems will be present under the mixed economy.

In evaluating a mixed economy it must be noted that there are areas of activity that prove unattractive to private investors e.g. investing in a fire service.

In addition if Government perceives that a given activity can grant too much economic power to the private sector Government will ensure control of it. e.g. the supply and distribution of water resources.

On occasions the full costs of an investment may be so high that Government is seen as being better able to supply it than leaving it to the private sector.

The nature of some activities also explains why Government would rather control them than leave it to the private sector e.g. Police Forces and Armies. One should have no difficulty in working out why Governments would not allow private defence forces or private police forces.

RESEARCH TASKS

1. What is the macro-economy?
2. List five resources of your own country.
3. Seek to discover resources in other countries.
4. Carefully assess the value of all the resources you have learnt about.
5. Give reasons with examples why specific institutions are permanently controlled by the State.

QUESTIONS

1. Select three resources of your country and show how they benefit your territory.
2. Select two resources of a country other than yours and prove their benefits to Caribbean economies.
3. Give three (3) reasons – with examples – why specific institutions are permanently controlled by the State.
4. Compare a free enterprise economy with a collectivist or planned economy.

CHAPTER 3

GETTING STARTED IN BUSINESS

A person who starts a business is called an entrepreneur. An entrepreneur is a risk-taker meaning that when he/she invests his/her money in the hope of making profits, he/she is taking a chance, and is in a way gambling. If the business proves unprofitable then being a risk-taker becomes quite clear. In a world where for everyone the future is uncertain, entrepreneurs may find out the hard way that the world of business and commerce is both uncertain and sometimes quite turbulent, and there is always the possibility that an investor could lose his/her money. For a start each entrepreneur must meet certain basic needs such as:

BASIC NEEDS

Land: This means somewhere – some physical location or space for the entrepreneur's operational and commercial activities.

Labour: Labour means workers. However some entrepreneurs in certain enterprises are able to operate as 'one-person' labour forces. Sole proprietors do all the work themselves. Consider vendors, hawkers, higglers, hucksters and the 'operators' of some shops. Many a cottage industry is owned and run by one person without any other person(s) serving as worker(s).

Capital: From a financial standpoint capital is the life-blood of every business. At the start of business, capital is absolutely necessary and before any inputs and assets are purchased it exists as money. Capital can either be fixed capital or working capital.

Many businesses have buildings, different kinds of technology and machines including automatic machines, plant and furniture. When money buys these things and is tied up in these business assets acquired via monetary investment, these things are described as fixed capital.

As a business continues in existence there are running costs such as monies needed to pay electricity, telephone bills, water, salaries and wages. Money is also needed for raw materials and factor inputs. Working capital is money needed to meet these current and recurrent costs.

Enterprise: Enterprise may be defined for current purposes as business initiative or acumen. This is the will and determination of the entrepreneur to get started in business. It always involves risk-taking.

DECISIONS EACH INDIVIDUAL ENTREPRENEUR MUST MAKE

(a) The type of business to operate and the products or services to produce.

(b) Requirements beyond land, labour and capital for the internal operations of the business.

(c) The source of raw materials and factor inputs.

(d) Location

(e) Number of workers.

(f) Types of workers.

(g) The quantity of capital after identifying the sources of capital.

(h) The kind of technology and machinery to use.

(i) The market - whether a market in their district or their own country, region or beyond.

(j) The kind of accounting system to use.

(k) The type of lending services required

(l) The types of insurance services to use.

(m) The type and amount of transport vehicles (if such are necessary)

(n) The types of shipping and freighting services to use when the business exports.

(o) Whether to make use of Government sponsored export credit.

(p) Whether to manage the business on a day to day basis or hire a manager.

(q) Whether to incorporate by forming a limited liability company.

(r) What type of internal organizational structure to use?

THE SOLE TRADER

This is a business person who provides all the capital needed and is a 'one-person' decision-maker. The business of the sole trader is unincorporated and has unlimited liability. It would be wrong to describe the business of the sole trader as a company. A business that cannot have Ltd. or Inc. at the end of its name is always unincorporated.

A sole trader's business is a firm but never a company.

Advantages of Operating as a Sole Trader

1. A sole trading establishment is quite easy to set up and except for things like basic trading licences and health certificates where applicable, there are no oppressive or expensive legal processes that must be gone through before setting up.

2. He or she can decide when to open and close the business.

3. In many sole trading businesses no huge amount of capital is necessary.

4. For a start the sole trader can be the sole worker in his business and depending on his or her circumstances can choose not to employ additional labour.

5. All profits belong to the owner.

6. Real world experience has shown that sole traders develop an intimate knowledge of their customers or clients and this could lead to goodwill for the sole trader.

7. The Sole Trader can determine which of his customers and clients can be trusted with credit. An intimate knowledge of customers will guide the sole trader as to which persons granted credit, might or might not repay.

Disadvantages of Operating as a Sole Trader

1. He or she might overwork.
2. He or she might close the business and be away at times when customers and clients need goods and services and then customers might go to a competitor and never do business with the sole trader again.
3. The sole trader might operate in an old fashioned way and prove to be inefficient.
4. When the sole trader needs capital especially working capital, his/her business can get into trouble.
5. All losses are borne by the sole trader.
6. By running an unincorporated business the personal property and belongings of the sole trader can be taken to satisfy the business debts of his or her business.
7. Many sole traders especially in the retail trades function in a business environment in which there is competition against them. Larger more efficient businesses could easily out- sell the sole trader.
8. The sole trader may find it hard to access capital especially in times of economic hardship.

On occasions some sole traders have decided to join up with other persons to put together resources and to continue to function in an unincorporated arrangement. When this happens a partnership comes into being.

WHY GO INTO BUSINESS

Different reasons influence different people to invest in business but as a general rule people enter business for the following purposes:

1. a desire for financial independence;
2. a desire to put their initiative into effect;
3. for self-fulfilment and self-actualization, meaning that entrepreneurs seek to derive a measure of psychological satisfaction from investing.

CHARACTERISTICS OF THE ENTREPRENEUR

The typical entrepreneur demonstrates the following qualities:

1. creativity;
2. risk taking;
3. innovation;
4. flexibility;
5. goal setting;
6. persistence and perseverance;
7. an opportunity to make a positive contribution to the wellbeing of the various stakeholders with whom he interacts.

STEPS FOR ESTABLISHING A BUSINESS

The first step involves undertaking a feasibility study. A feasibility study raises the question how possible or practicable it is to launch a business. Issues to be taken into account are the following:

1. To what market should goods and services produced be aimed?
2. What is the true market size?
3. Specifically what goods and services ought to be produced?
4. What impact does existing competition have on the plans of the entrepreneur to produce?
5. Is there a need for market research?
6. Specifically what type of market research should be undertaken?
7. Should the entrepreneur seek out business associates to join with him in commencing business?
8. Specifically what particular type of business should be operated: should it be a sole trader's business, a partnership, a private company or a public company?
9. Would the entrepreneur's business be in need of technical staff and specialists?

After the entrepreneur has carefully pursued his feasibility study he ought to then move on to a business plan. The first item in the business plan should cover the legal steps required to set up business whether a trading licence, the incorporation of the firm and such like (bear in mind that the legal formalities depend heavily on the type of business to be established).

Items in the business plan include

1. The capital necessary at the start and in the medium term.
2. The size and type of business operation to set up in terms of the structure of the business.
3. The vision, mission, goals and objectives of the business.
4. The constraints or challenges the business is likely to face.
5. The type of banking services and insurance services needed.
6. The type of transport needed.
7. The kind of opening hours the business would establish.
8. Any linkages with existing firms.
9. The nature of mechanization and automation which may be necessary.
10. The firm's organizational chart involving production, personnel, marketing and finance.

FUNCTIONAL AREAS

It is for the entrepreneur to decide what particular departments he would set up. A range of departments exist in the real world such as personnel, production, marketing, finance, legal, research and development and such like.

OTHER FACTORS TO BE CONSIDERED BY THE ENTREPRENEUR

At the very start of his business the entrepreneur needs to figure out whether conducting market research is desirable.

The entrepreneur will realize that in some measure his feasibility study would be somewhat related to his business plan. He must remember that both his feasibility study and his business plan will raise the issue of sources and types of capital as well as how to operate.

OTHER IMPORTANT FACTORS

At the start of his business the entrepreneur has to be clear as to what government's business policies are. For example, would he have to get some special licence beyond a mere trading licence? Would there be any environmental issues which he has to face?

He would have to be aware of what types of taxes are required by government and the level of these taxes. Dependent on the type of business the entrepreneur operates, he and his planners (where such exist) should be aware of the fact that issues such as misleading advertisements, tax evasion, the indiscriminate disposal of waste and money laundering are forbidden.

RESEARCH TASKS

1. Why are some businesses called 'firms' and others are styled companies or corporations?
2. Seek to discover the distinction between the Private Sector and the Public Sector.
3. Do the goals of the Public Sector ever closely resemble those of the Private Sector?
4. List four (4) social and economic benefits which the Private Sector can provide for society.
5. (a) What is meant by the informal sector?
   (b) Why do some people function in the informal sector?
   (c) What problems may be presented by members of the informal sector?
6. Research environmental impact processes

QUESTIONS

1. Identify two factors of production.
2. Suggest reasons why these factors of production are important.
3. What are raw materials?
4. Indicate five decisions each entrepreneur has to make.
5. Assess the importance of these decisions

CHAPTER 4

THE NATURE OF BUSINESS

WHAT IS BUSINESS

Business activity relates to the production, purchase and exchange of goods and services. There are in practice other activities for example banking, insurance, advertising and transport which are closely related to business activity and which support such activity. These four areas are themselves businesses as well. If one considers how all businesses are started then the idea of enterprise has to be appreciated. Other business concepts have to be understood as well.

ENTERPRISE

A dictionary definition of enterprise suggests that it is:-

> (a) Initiative in business.
> (b) Readiness to embark on new ventures.
> (c) The courage or effort required to set out on an undertaking or project.

All three of the above can be taken together as making up enterprise.

However, there is a second meaning to the word 'Enterprise' where this noun can be used to refer to a business undertaking, entity or organization.

In practice the person or persons who put their enterprise to the test venture out into a future that is uncertain at the time of the initial investment.

Those who decide to put their sense of enterprise into effect are known as entrepreneurs.

ENTREPRENEURSHIP

Entrepreneurship refers to the actions of the entrepreneur.

The entrepreneur who is a risk-taker provides the initiative out of which an enterprise is created. Merely providing the initiative to start a business, though very important, is not all the functions of the entrepreneur. But other areas will now be first examined.

GROSS PROFIT

Some writers define profit as the net gain made from the sale of goods and services.

However, it is necessary to note that every business incurs expenses so the best way of defining profit is the gain made when all expenses are deducted from trading income and sales.

Gross profit is the difference between what goods and services are sold for and the cost price of these goods and services. So if a seller receives $35,000 after taking out the cost of sales, gross profit is in issue.

Net profit is the result after each and every expense like advertising, utilities and transport has been deducted from the gross profit.

In some countries the net profit of businesses is taxable at going taxation rate on profits.

LOSSES

In cases where a firm's total expenses are higher than its income, then the firm will be operating at a loss.

A reasonable question to consider is whether a firm after achieving a gross profit can incur a loss.

So long as rent, cost of utilities, cost of transport, advertising and transport and other expenses have when all added up, reduced the gross profit to zero or below zero then losses are in evidence.

TRADE AND COMMERCE

Trade and commerce involve exchange. In today's world sellers market their goods and services usually in exchange for money.

Trade occurs at various levels.

Home Trade
Import Trade
Export Trade also exists and affects Caribbean territories.

Home trade or domestic trade is strictly commerce restricted to within the boundaries of a given territory.

In a modern world there are different types of Trade and trade is a feature in any economy.

ORGANIZATIONS IN COMMERCE AND TRADE

The world of business and trade is affected by different organizations, for example, banks and insurance companies feature in the national economy for reasons that would become clear in future chapters but trade involves exchange and in today's world many an instrument representing money is used.

Readers should note that there can be trade in tangibles (goods) or intangibles (services) and must be aware that some writers refer to goods as commodities.

History has taught us that as human-kind learned how to manipulate his/her environment, there came a point when specialization and the division of labour led to goods being produced more quickly and better in quality.

MODERN DEVELOPMENTS

In recent years, credit cards which are triggered electronically have been used in businesses and trade, and through telegraphic transfers and other electronic transfers payments can be made faster than by old fashioned methods. Readers are also asked to note that computers have allowed for the evolution of E-commerce.

Whatever the world's modern developments most people establish businesses in the expectation of increasing their wealth.

Among the persons seeking profits and wealth are:

(a) Entrepreneurs.
(b) Shareholders in enterprises.
(c) Citizens who deposit money in savings accounts, time and fixed deposits and savings bonds.
(d) Purchasers of mutual funds.
(e) Those who buy life insurance policies.
(f) Purchasers of pension plans.
(g) Investors in credit union programmes.

RESEARCH TASKS

1. Look to ascertain any difference which may exist between 'profit' and 'wealth.'
2. Identify ten different types of enterprises in the public and private sectors in the Caribbean.
3. Under what circumstances would barter be used in these modern times?
4. Chambers of Commerce exist throughout the Caribbean. Evaluate the part played by these bodies.
5. What does 'E-Commerce' entail and what are its advantages?

QUESTIONS

1. Explain the difference between an Entrepreneur and a Manager.
2. In what circumstance(s) would an Entrepreneur and Manager be one and the same person.
3. Distinguish between fixed capital and working capital.
4. Suggest two reasons why working capital is very important.
5. Provide two examples of fixed assets

CHAPTER 5

TYPES OF BUSINESS UNITS

THE SOLE TRADER

A Sole Trader is a person who is in business by himself or herself.

The Sole Trader is his or her own 'one person' entrepreneur and therefore bears all associated risks alone.

Generally, the sole trader provides all of the capital for the business and many a sole trader also provides his own labour directly and without the help of others.

Advantages of Operating as a Sole Trader

1. Is free to open and close as he/she wishes.
2. Offers personalized service.
3. No elaborate regulations stand in the way of operating as a Sole Trader.
4. Can generate enormous goodwill by being present to render service or sell goods to customers.
5. Can decide on which customers are credit worthy.
6. Is free to keep all profits.

Disadvantages

1. May end up working very, very long hours and is faced by fatigue and exhaustion.
2. Many Sole Traders are so old-fashioned as not to make use of modern technology.
3. If the Sole Trader is ill or unavailable his/her business will be closed.

Sole Traders have to bear unlimited liability which means that a sole trader's personal property that has no link to the business is at risk if the business gets into heavy debt or cannot meet its payments.

Finally, Sole traders bear all the losses of their businesses.

PARTNERSHIPS

General

Partnerships except for limited partnerships normally have between two and twenty members or partners. Partnerships are relatively easy to form and in this respect resemble the sole trader's type of business. In the absence of a partnership agreement, profits are shared equally.

Advantages

1. Where more than one person joins with others it can be taken that more capital becomes available. In nearly every partnership, individual partners would be expected to provide capital.
2. Some partners might bring specialist skills to the partnership which would bring benefits to the partnership.
3. Partners can share responsibilities by rotating and rostering times and schedules and work-loads.
4. Partners are free to run their business according to the wishes of the partners as a whole.
5. Partnerships are very easy to set up.

Disadvantages

1. There can be conflict among partners. Many partners come together not having properly decided on the details of the partnership so that there may be squabbles among the partners not just over money, but also over methods of operating.
2. Like sole traders, partnerships carry unlimited liability.
3. Partners are individually and collectively responsible for the debts of their business.

A special word about limited partnerships.

Limited partnerships are rare but with a limited partnership at least one partner must have unlimited liability. What this means is that in this type of partnership legal provision is made for one or more partners to limit their liability up to the amounts of capital that they have invested in the business. A limited partnership is an example of an enterprise which combines the characteristics of the sole trader with the other type of business unit. However, as indicated previously limited partnerships are rare.

CO-OPERATIVES

Years ago, many a Caribbean Co-operative carried unlimited liability; but in recent years Co-operatives have been permitted limited liability status so that those involved in co-operatives will not be at risk of losing personal property to satisfy the debts of the co-operatives but will have only to face the prospect of losing what they have invested in the co-operatives.

In the Caribbean there are co-operatives such as Fisherman's Co-operatives, Farmers Co-operatives and Financial Co-operatives which are also known as credit unions.

Co-operatives are based on the principle of open membership and fraternity and historically they have practiced democratic control by allowing for one vote per member. Co-operatives also rank all members equally. Another traditional principle pursued by Co-operatives is that the welfare of members takes precedence over considerations like profit. In fact, excess money made in Co-operatives is normally called surplus and not profits, the idea being that people matter more than money.

COMPANIES

A company is a business unit which is in itself and of itself its own separate legal entity. Companies are said to have their own legal personalities. For example, a company can sue and be sued in its own name.

A company is said to have limited liability meaning that persons who have invested funds in limited liability companies are only responsible for the money they have invested or agreed to invest in these limited liability companies. But individuals who invest in these companies do not stand to lose any personal property at all. Personal property stands separate from the amounts of money they have pledged to put in companies or have actually put in companies. For example, John has $10,000. He puts $5,000 in ABC Ltd. and banks the remaining $5,000. If ABC Ltd. sets into any kind of trouble and is sued, John is only responsible or better still can only lose the $5,000 he has actually invested whereas, the balance of the funds held to his account in the bank remains John's personal property and is not at risk to satisfy the debts of ABC Ltd.

Vindra has agreed by contract to invest $12,000 in DEF Ltd. She is yet to put in the money into this company but understands that she is under a contractual duty to put in the $12,000 in DEF Ltd. She would only be responsible in law for the amount that she has pledged to invest in the company.

It is important to note that an investor in a company and the company itself are two separate and different legal beings. Some writers say that companies have artificial legal personalities.

Another feature of companies is that their name must end either with the letters 'Ltd.' or 'Inc.'. Ltd. means Limited and indicates that the company's liabilities are limited to the amounts put in by investors while Inc. means that the entity is incorporated as its own legal person. Indeed entities whose names end in 'Limited' are also incorporated entities. A few companies have PLC in place of Ltd. or Inc. PLC means public limited companies.

PRIVATE LIMITED COMPANIES

Nowadays, the best definition which can be given to a private company is that it is a business organization which is not allowed to buy and sell shares publicly. Historically, private companies used to have between two and fifty shareholders but the law has changed considerably in some territories. However, the law still allows for some companies to make arrangements by which they settle capital matters privately.

A public company is one which is allowed to trade its shares (buying and selling shares) publicly. This means that a public company can advertise to the public asking members of the public to bring money to it in exchange for shares. It also means that where a public company has been permitted to become a listed company on a stock exchange that it can use the medium of the stock exchange for the purchase and sale of its shares.

THE PROSPECTUS

To become a public limited company, a company must produce a prospectus which provides details about the conduct of its business. This will include its trading activities and the financial documents of the business such as its Profit & Loss Statement and its Balance Sheet. This allows potential investors to be aware of the viability of the company and thus be in a position to make a sound business decision.

MORE ABOUT COMPANIES

One of the biggest attractions to forming companies is that the concept of limited liability or separate incorporation permits shareholders the psychological comfort of knowing that they can hold onto their personal private property even when the company in which they have put money goes bankrupt. But there are other characteristics about companies that need to be noted.

HOLDING COMPANIES

A Holding Company is a company that owns other companies. The normal situation is for the holding company to raise substantial amounts of capital while at the same time permitting individual companies to come under its umbrella. Holding Companies can be said to be owners of subsidiary companies.

CONGLOMERATES

In one sense a conglomerate is an umbrella corporation or company which brings together several different companies under its umbrella. Many holding companies end up being conglomerate. In a second sense there could be many different companies or legal entities which are controlled by a headquartered type company which 'merges' them either for convenience or for administration.

MULTINATIONALS

A multinational is a company which locates its branches in many different nations or territories. One of the well known multinationals that has come into existence in recent times is the First Caribbean Bank but the Caribbean has known multinational agencies like Berger Paints, Goddards and others.

RESEARCH TASKS

1. Find out what incorporation entails.
2. Locate examples of unincorporated businesses.
3. Compare and contrast 'firm' and 'company'.
4. Research
   (a)   The concept of prospectus.
   (b)   Stock Exchanges.
5. Collect as much information as possible on:
   (a)   Multinationals.
   (b)   Conglomerates.
   (c)   Holding Companies.
   (d)   Subsidiaries.

QUESTIONS

1. List three examples of benefits a person can achieve by operating as a sole trader.
2. List two disadvantages in operating as a sole trader.
3. Jimmy Deodorine has been a successful sole trader for ten years and seeks your advice as to whether he should convert his business to a partnership.
   a. Provide thorough advice to Jimmy before he makes the change to a partnership.
   b. Explain with examples the differences between unlimited liability and limited liability.
   c. What is meant by 'separate legal entity'?

CHAPTER 6

PRODUCTION

DEFINITION OF PRODUCTION

Production is the manner or process by which something is created or made. Depending on the nature of the goods and services which are to be produced, making a product can be easy or complex.

DIRECT PRODUCTION

Under a system of direct production the producer and consumer tend to be one and the same person or one and the same group. Direct production entails the consumer's production of a good and sometimes a service for his or her own use with no trade or commerce involved.

Direct production under a subsistence system can mobilize families and even communities to work together and to save but there are some important questions that are always relevant.

Consider the following:

1. Would each person have all the time to produce all his/her needs and wants?
2. Would everybody have the skill(s) to produce everything on his/her own?
3. Where manufacturing and construction are concerned, which both involve scores and scores of inputs and raw materials, would each individual be able to locate all the resources to source and create raw materials and factor inputs?
4. If direct production were the norm nowadays what would the quality of goods and services be like?
5. Could modern inventions like large ships, computers, aircraft and sophisticated machinery and automatic equipment have been created under a system of direct production?

For reasons which the average keen reader could easily calculate, direct production has largely given way to indirect production.

INDIRECT PRODUCTION

Indirect production is a system by which specialist producers create or make goods and services available to consumers.

Its existence has contributed immensely to modern trade and commerce.

Indirect production makes use of specialization and the division of labour. Specialization encourages experimentation, creativity and initiative and drives the profit motive.

Under the system of modern commercial (indirect) production much of which takes place in highly competitive business environments, production is complete when the goods and services are in the hands of their final consumers. Expressed another way production is completed when goods and services reach the market.

SPECIALIZATION

Specialization and the Division of Labour

Here reference is made to 'breaking down' tasks in ways where rather than one worker completely finishing given tasks, production is organized by assigning different workers to different tasks.

Advantages of Specialization

1. Workers show more skill and expertise in their jobs.
2. Tasks become easier to handle.
3. With the division of labour the total productivity of each worker increases.
4. Costs per unit are lower.
5. Under specialization machinery, equipment and automatic equipment can be better utilized.

Disadvantages of Specialization

1. Doing the same job over and over again becomes monotonous.
2. Where machines are used the role of workers may be reduced through mechanization and automation.
3. The constant increasing use of machines can cause workers to be made redundant.
4. Productivity and production are affected if slower workers on the production line keep back production by functioning too tardily.

MASS PRODUCTION

Mass production occurs when goods are produced in enormous quantities.

For mass production to be achieved mechanization and moreso automation are used extensively with the aim of keeping down production costs while producing in large volumes.

As labour costs may be high care is taken to ensure both that workers offer the greatest levels of productivity possible while making use of specialist workers, capable of operating the machinery (including automated machines).

One of the objectives of mass production is the reduction of costs per unit of production and this is so since the firm would wish to offer cheaper products to the community and be able to offer competitive prices in the market place.

Units and component parts which are exploited and put into the process of production are often made to carry standardized sizes and specifications since the objective is to avoid high production costs.

Specialization and the division of labour represent some of the characteristics of mass production and workers are usually of a special type. Indeed workers who function in a mass production environment not only tend to be specialists but work closely and intensively with machines and equipment.

There is little room available for unskilled labour in plants and businesses which practice mass production.

The benefits of mass production tend to be:-
　　(a) speed in the production process.
　　(b) Uniformity of products which are made (standardization).
　　(c) Efficiency in production.
　　(d) A reduction in costs per unit.
　　(e) The production of technical and specialized equipment and goods.

Where the costs of production are kept down to a minimum, the producer exploiting mass production can go to the market with cheaper goods thereby being able to compete as far as pricing is concerned.

One of the drawbacks of mass production is the relatively high startup costs of installing very expensive equipment.

Another drawback occurs when the machines breakdown thereby halting production.

The costs associated with maintaining the machinery tend to be high.

Yet mass production may be desirable. However since Caribbean populations and unemployment levels tend to be high organized labour would be concerned when businesses convert from being labour intensive to capital intensive.

Under mass production skilled specialists gain opportunities from employment and go on to function in capital intensive industries in a Caribbean environment in which there is scope and need for work opportunities for unskilled and semi-skilled labour.

PRODUCTIVITY

Productivity relates to the effectiveness and efficiency in the production process. Productivity is about the capacity to produce. Productivity measures the rate of output compared to the units of input

Factors that affect the efficiency of labour

1. The level of training of the work force and the skills of workers.
2. The general health and safety of workers at work.
3. The conditions, physical and otherwise in the workplace.
4. The quality and attitude of supervision and management.
5. The health of the workers.
6. How workers function as part of a team.
7. The speed with which work is done.
8. The quality work actually produced.

MIGRATION

Migration literally means movement. Movement into a country from outside is known as immigration. Movement from a country to go abroad is known as emigration.

FACTORS THAT AFFECT IMMIGRATION

1. Entry into the country because one's workplace has moved into the country.
2. Entry into the country to work in technical areas in support of the country to which the emigrant has moved.
3. Seeking job prospects and a better quality of life in the new country.

The above are pull factors which would normally operate to entice people to come to the Caribbean territories. However, it seems to be the case that more Caribbean nationals emigrate to larger richer nations than do other people come into the Caribbean.

PUSH FACTORS THAT EXPLAIN EMIGRATION:

1. High levels of unemployment among the poor.
2. The strongly held view that economic and social conditions in Caribbean countries would not improve.
3. There is a corps of Caribbean nationals who are very highly trained and qualified but are underpaid and so these people leave in search of higher incomes and a better quality of life.
4. Many Caribbean nationals leave to join family and friends.
5. Persons who are highly intelligent but have no faith in their countries of origin emigrate in search of a better life. This is what is called the brain drain.

FACTORS OF PRODUCTION

The four factors of production are
1. Land
2. Labour
3. Capital
4. Enterprise

Land

Land, the raw earth, things attached to the land and natural resources growing in the land or found on lands are usually described simply as land.

While it is true that a farmer needs land to grow his or her produce, there are persons who are not farmers who still need space on which or in which they can operate their businesses. Even hawkers, hucksters and higglers need space. In economics 'space' can be considered as 'land'.

Labour

Human effort is needed to facilitate production. Indeed workers are hired for their productivity (capacity to produce efficiently). Most work sites need workers. 'Labour' is used to describe those who work. Human skill and effort are needed to get production going.

Capital

There are occasions when 'capital' simply means investment finance or money to be applied in the production process, but machinery, plant and equipment are sometimes known as capital. Like land and labour (and enterprise) capital is important for business activity. Capital, can for a start, be treated as money invested in business taking into account the fact that small business people who do not operate nor own machinery, still need some capital to get going in business.

Enterprise

For present purposes Enterprise can be described as all those qualities linked to the decision to take a risk or risks to launch a business even where the future is uncertain. These include:
1. Planning the creation of a business
2. Conceptualizing the format of a business.
3. Reassessing and reevaluating the plans for the business.
4. Locating finance and capital for the start-up of the business.
5. Developing a clear business plan.
6. Deciding how to organize the business.
7. Deciding how to operate the business.
8. Coordinating the factors of production.

The entrepreneur will in practice be an innovative, persistent individual who has set goals and objectives based on a clear mission.

TYPES OF PRODUCTION

As far as the nature of production is concerned there are four basic types of production. These are treated below.

Extractive Production

Some production is called extractive or primary production. Goods and products in their raw and natural state are said to exist at the extractive stage of production. So raw fish taken from the seas, rivers and lakes would be at the extractive stage of production. Similarly, raw carrots, beets and potatoes are goods and commodities that exist at the extractive stage of production. The reason why some writers call extractive production primary production is because goods and products which are mined, fished for or harvested without undergoing any change or any refining, can be taken to be at the very first or primary stage of production.

Construction

Construction which is concerned with building represents its own special type of production and so where structures are built whether as houses or as hotels or buildings reserved for manufacturing these would be classified under construction. Construction is secondary production.

Manufacturing

Another type of production is manufacturing or industrial production which is concerned with converting raw materials into a higher stage of production. Manufacturing is concerned with the making of products whether through assembly, raw materials or component parts into finished goods or even doing such things as canning carrots, beets or other agricultural commodities. Manufacturing is referred to as secondary production, meaning that production has been taken a stage higher than primary production.

Production of Services

A fourth type of production is the production of services. The production of services referred to as tertiary production provides amenity, comfort and satisfaction to clients without necessarily putting something in the clients' hands or mouths. The production of services involves such things as transport, banking and insurance. Tourism is also a service.

COTTAGE INDUSTRIES

A cottage industry is a manufacturing plant set up in the home of its entrepreneur.

Characteristics of Cottage Industries

1. There is no need to invest in a building or to have to pay rent.
2. Labour costs can be kept to a minimum since the entrepreneur can use the labour of family members.
3. Cottage industries allow for the skills and talents of their operators to find expression.
4. Neither large nor substantial capital outlay is necessary.
5. Many operators of cottage industries make jams and jellies, art and craft, condiments, pepper sauces, indigenous confectionery and the like

Practical experience has shown that the operators of cottage industries are very discreet when it comes to marketing their produce. For example, some entrepreneurs in cottage industries sell their products to local hotels thereby creating a forward link with the tourism sector.

LINKAGE INDUSTRIES

Consider these scenarios:

John makes building blocks and after four years in the business bought out a quarry and a business that produces cement. The fact that John was at a higher level of production than the two businesses he bought out and went backwards down the "production lines" shows that John established backward linkages. A backward linkage is therefore one which comes about when a producer goes backwards and links his business to others.

FORWARD LINKAGES

Josiah Ramlogan has a huge kitchen garden and sells half of his produce to a local supermarket and the balance to a hotel in his vicinity. The fact that Josiah is moving up the production process and linking his business to two businesses shows that Josiah is taking his produce forward and in the process establishes a forward linkage.

A forward linkage is therefore linking of a business which is lower down the production chain to one which is higher up.

LOCATION OF BUSINESSES

One of the decisions which any producer has to make is where to locate. The location of a business may bring very special benefits to that business. Many years ago, it was fashionable to speak of localization, meaning that business was located based on some special characteristic of the locale or locality where producers established their business. Modern developments in transport, in the manufacture of specially designed and equipped motor vehicles and machinery, and the availability of flexible forms of transport have in great measure undermined the localization theory. Yet in some measure there could still be advantages in selecting an appropriate location.

Factors that influence the Location of business

1. Closeness to the supply of raw materials.
2. Closeness to airports and seaports.
3. Closeness to the market.
4. Closeness to sources of labour.
5. Closeness to or presence in centrally located areas such as cities and towns.
6   Ready access to information technology

THE SMALL FIRM AND GROWTH

THE SMALL FIRM

Advantages of Small Firms

The small firm can present some positive facts in its favour; for example, if the small firm is located in a remote village it can do the following:

1. Provide goods and services to the locality and in the process prevent residents from having to travel far to cities.
2. With most small firms, no huge amounts of capital are necessary.
3. The small firm can also produce and sell special items which allow people to access them in a convenient way.
4. The small firm can offer personalized service and in the process attract goodwill.
5. Many small firms can provide speed of service to customers especially in small villages.
6. Many small firms demonstrate the same advantages as cottage industries and sole proprietorships.

Disadvantages of Small Firms

The small firm may not be able to control unit costs and keep prices down.

Practical experience has shown that the goods and services of larger firms are cheaper than those of smaller firms.

While larger firms can present and benefit from economies of scale and economies of scope, small firms are not in a position to experience such advantages.

The operators of some small firms may lack proper accounting and management skills.

Many small firms find it hard to raise capital.

IMPLICATIONS OF GROWTH

When a small business decides to expand or take on more, many issues arise. Firstly, the business will find that it would need more capital; secondly, the business will find that it needs to identify more markets; and thirdly, a business moving from small and micro status will find the need for more labour, sometimes skilled labour. As a firm grows, attention has to be paid to how the firm is structured and organized internally.

In this day and age money would have to be found to invest in appropriate technology.

ADVANTAGES OF GROWTH

The business can decide on a greater product range with proper plans in place and well-structured functional line departments and there is a strong probability that it may be able for the first time to decrease cost per unit thereby making it easier to compete. The changed business may also find that it would be easier to achieve economies of scale.

Problems Associated with Growth

Some of the problems associated with growth of a firm may centre on the following:

- Attracting new capital may be difficult and costly.
- Money will have to be found to train new workers.
- The cost of labour may increase.

The management of the small firm could have been extremely efficient running a small firm but then as the firm grows the manager could find it extremely difficult to manage a bigger firm.

LABOUR INTENSIVE INDUSTRIES

A Labour Intensive Industry is one which needs and makes use of great amounts of labour, usually unskilled labour. Before mechanization the sugarcane industry at the level of field operations made use of much unskilled labour. Caribbean populations tend to be large so labour intensive industries would be welcome to provide working opportunities to persons who may otherwise have been unemployed.

Nowadays tourism is seen as a labour intensive business and the many data processing firms which have come to the Caribbean employ large amounts of labour.

CAPITAL INTENSIVE INDUSTRIES

Capital Intensive Industries make use of much technology and machinery. When a business shifts from being labour intensive to capital intensive workers are often made redundant.

One important feature of Capital Intensive Industries is that they tend to employ specialist labour or highly skilled labour.

RESEARCH TASKS

1.   Distinguish between 'level of production' and 'type of production'.
2.   Carefully research with examples the concept of 'linkage' industries.
3.   Research the possible contribution which small businesses can make.
4.   Indicate how a sole trader's business is established compared with a private limited company.
5.   Carefully research the concept of organised labour.
6.   Why do many workers seek representation?
7.   What is the likely attitude of organized labour to a business which is changing from labour intensive to capital intensive?

QUESTIONS

1.   Explain the concept of indirect production.
2.   Carefully define specialization and the division of labour.
3.   Carol Singh runs a farm of three acres in size. Generally on occasions Carol is faced with serious challenges.
        Suggest two possible difficulties that Carol would face as a farmer.
4.   Comparing a manufacturer with the producer of agricultural commodities what are the challenges faced by a farmer which do not confront a manufacturer?
5.   Suggest three disadvantages which result from specialization.
6.   Identify three factors which affect the efficiency of labour.
        Why do these factors affect the efficiency of labour?

CHAPTER 7

INTERNAL ORGANIZATIONAL ENVIRONMENT

SOME GENERAL POINTERS

As far as the organizational structure of a firm is concerned different organizations present differing structures. However before examining actual structures in detail the two concepts below must be understood. These are:

> (a) The Chain of Command; and
> (b) The Span of Management often labeled the Span of Control.

The Chain of Command may exist as a Pyramid with layers of power and authority. Consider the pyramid below:

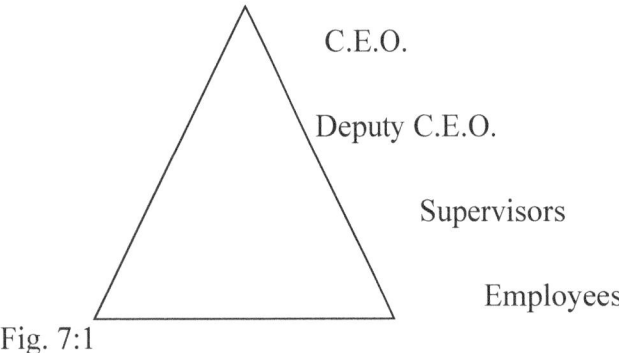

C.E.O.

Deputy C.E.O.

Supervisors

Employees

Fig. 7:1

Those at the top of the pyramid have more power and authority than those who occupy the lower rungs.

SPAN OF MANAGEMENT/SPAN OF CONTROL

This refers to the numbers who work under Management. For example if Deodrine is manager of ZPT Ltd. and fifty people work under him, the span of management or control is thereby realised. This is a wide span of control

Where it is necessary for to be closely supervised, the span of control will be narrow.

Conversely where workers do not have to be supervised closely, the span of management and control will be wide.

Highly relevant to the idea of Span of Control/Management are:-
> • Some tasks are so easy as to require minimum supervision.

- Some workers are responsible and so self-motivated as not to need   .
- Some managers, dependent on their personal qualities and capacity to control matters so attract the cooperation of their subordinates, that they do not need narrow spans of control.

SPAN OF CONTROL

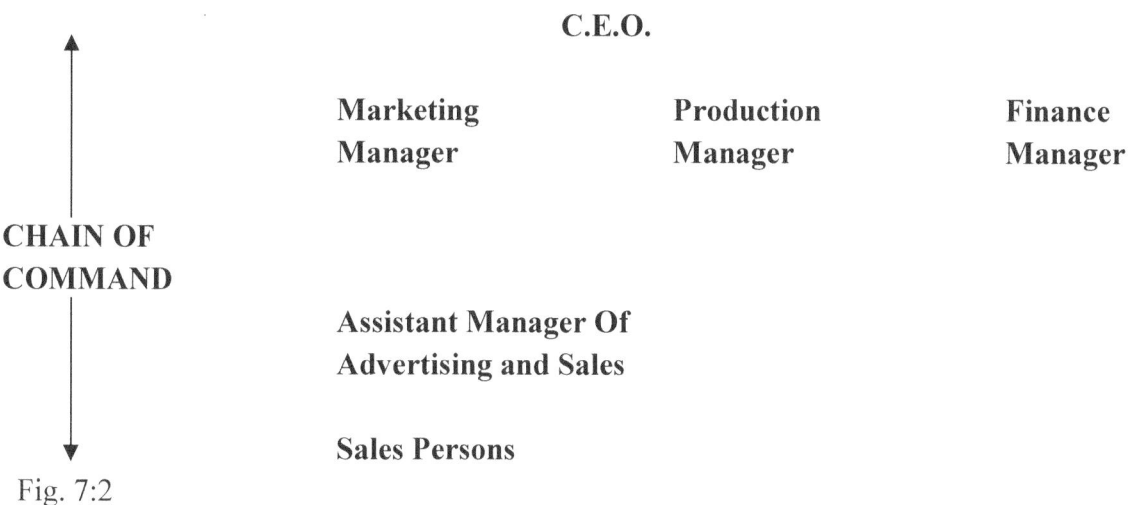

Fig. 7:2

In figure 7.2 the span of control is demonstrated in the relationship between the CEO and the three Managers (Marketing, Production, and Finance). There is a narrow span of control. The Chain of command is represented by the line relationship from the CEO to the Marketing Manager, to the Assistant Manager of Advertising and Sales and then to the Sales personnel.

A WIDE SPAN OF CONTROL

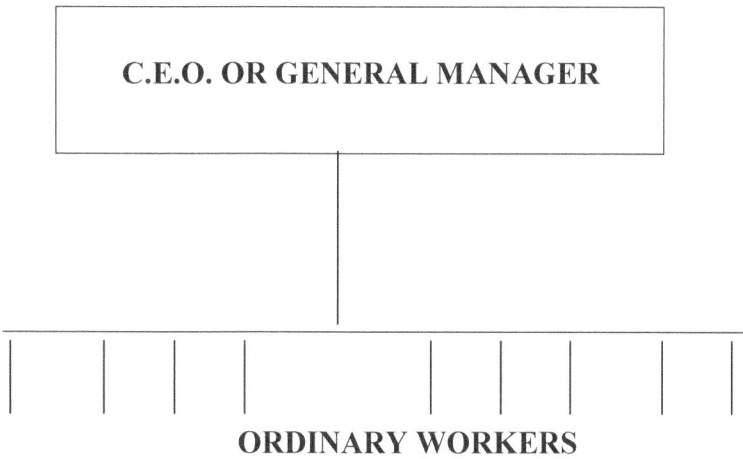

Fig. 7:3

This figure (7.3) shows a wide span of control with many workers supervised by one person. There are four basic types of organization structure and on occasions there is a combination of more than one matrix or structure, meaning that rather than have a single 'pure' structure element(s) from other structures are incorporated either into each other or in concert with a different chart.

The four basic types of organizational structure are:

(a)   Committee organization
(b)   Functional Organisation.
(c)   Line Organisation.
(d)   Line and Staff Organisation.

THE COMMITTEE ORGANISATION

This type of organisation's philosophy is that the grouping of experts and specialists in Committees to advise Management will lead to meaningful and effective decision-making.

The primary purpose of the committee type organization is for subordinates to advise supervisors (their superiors). Where persons lower down the ladder advise those who occupy the upper echelons, there is said to be upward communication.

Committees may be brought together temporarily for specific purposes or they may be permanently appointed to work and advise on policy.

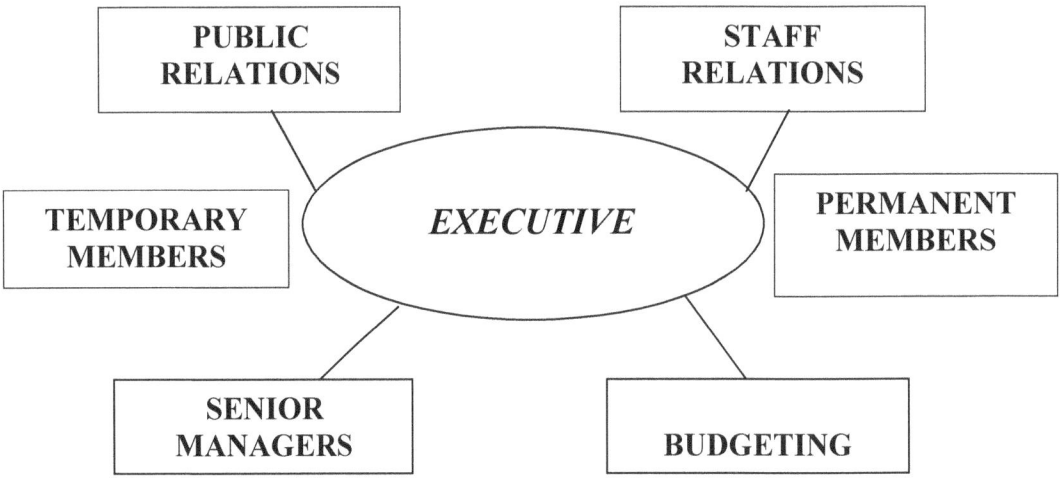

The above represents the Committee System – Fig. 7:4

THE LINE ORGANISATION

Consider the diagram below:

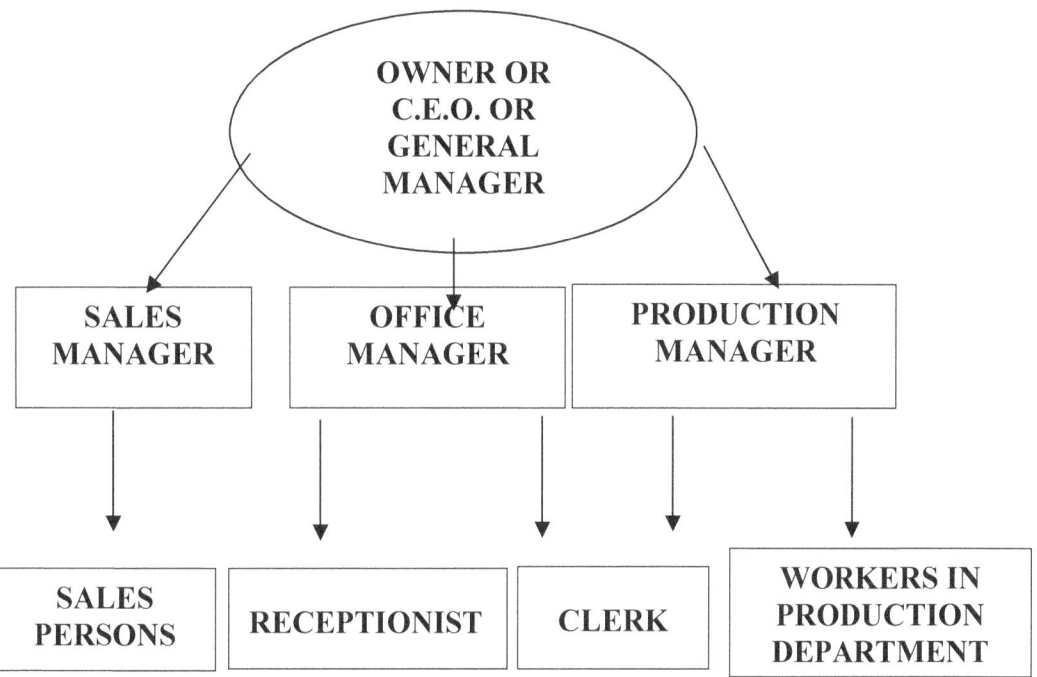

Fig 7.5

As a general rule Line Organisation exhibits and demonstrates a direct flow of authority. The 'boss' gives directives to those subordinates whom he supervises. Where his supervisors themselves have subordinates these supervisors are expected to carry out the wishes of the boss (C.E.O.) by giving the appropriate instructions to those below.

A feature of Line Organisation is the higher up the organisation's ladder the greater the authority so to this extent there is resemblance to the pyramid.

Under this system where a functionary bears particular responsibilities he or she cannot pass it on to others.

The Line Organisation exhibits a straight forward chain of command permitting decisions to be reached expeditiously but the C.E.O. is kept busy interfacing with his middle managers and supervisors.

Doubts have been expressed over whether the line organization actually allows for there to be specialists who can be assigned to more than one department.

FUNCTIONAL ORGANISATION

Now consider the following:

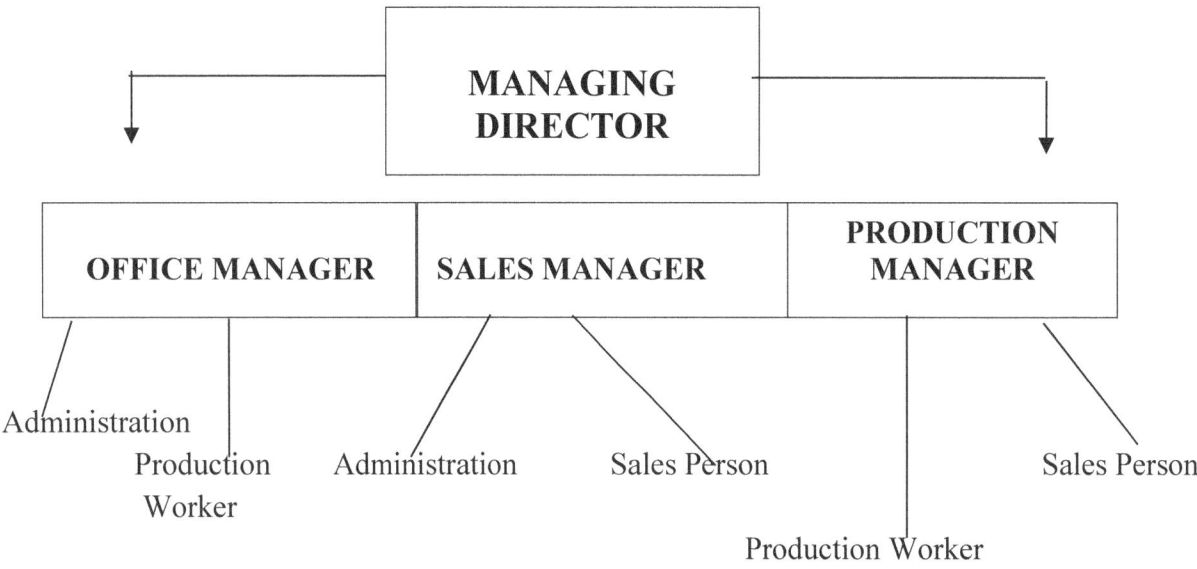

Fig 7.6

Under the system of functional organization the business entity is characterized by the division of the business into specific functions.

There are individual departmental heads supervising staff, but also interfacing closely with each other.

In other words managers and supervisors of departments communicate with each other in matters pertinent to their own specific functions.

As far as functional organization is concerned, within the various departments instructions are passed on to employees who present periodic reports on their activities.

This leads to regular communication and builds trust.

LINE AND STAFF ORGANISATION

This type of organization combines the line organization with the staff organization.

Here the actual objectives of the entity are brought into effect as though they are in the line organization.

Lines of authority are kept clear. The line and staff organization combines the line organization with the functional organization. Under the Line and Staff Organisation, the objectives of the firm are put into effect as if they are in a Line Organisation.

With it the Chief Executive Officer holds many meetings with departmental heads with the aim of clarifying and effecting their entity's policies, programmes and activities.

So long as Heads of Departments understand their functions as communicated to them by the C.E.O. lines of authority are put into effect not only to achieve the firm's goals but also to allow for greater coordination among departments.

Feedback occurs frequently and trust is built:

between C.E.O. and Senior Supervisor and Managers; Senior Supervisors and Managers on the one hand and ordinary subordinate workers on the other hand.

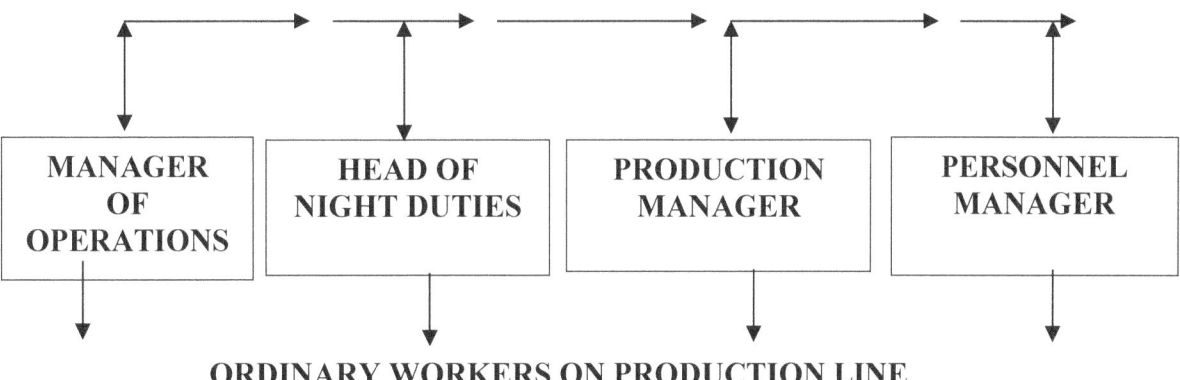

Fig. 7:7

MANAGEMENT INFORMATION SYSTEMS

There are four types of Management Information Systems in operation.

These are:
(a)   Transaction Processing Systems;
(b)   Decision-Making Support Systems;
(c)   Office Automation Systems; and
(d)   Executive Support Systems.

1. **Transaction Processing Systems** do the following:

Process Orders.
Handle Point of Sale transactions.
Aid supermarkets, gasoline stations, mini-marts and other businesses.
Exist primarily as automatic teller machines which allow cashiers to ring in data and
    receive outputs of information as well.

2.   **Decision-Making Support Systems**

With potential for complexities, decision-making support systems are used to facilitate decision-making. Since there are scores and scores of decisions which have to be made, some on a daily basis, standardization of methods and techniques under this particular system is difficult to introduce.

3.   **Office Automation Systems**

The principal role of Office Automation Systems is to facilitate and expedite communication with the firm. The system is geared to exploit multi-media systems and things like voice and video communications are available under office automation systems. Data Processing, Illustrations and Graphics are also available under the office automation system.

The systems also cater to electronic mail, image processing and voice mail.

4.   **Executive Support Systems**

In many firms standardised information and materials have proved necessary to assist executives in decision-making. The executive support system is made use of by supervisors, middle managers and senior executives.

The overall advantages available from the use of the MIS systems dealt with above are:

1. Facilitating communications and decision-making.
2. Allowing for the storage and retrieval of important data.
3. Saving of time while enhancing productivity.
4. Allowing standardized procedures for the execution of a wide range of activities.
5. Saving space and paper
6. The amalgamation of the mechanism(s) for monitoring and maintaining specific activities.
7. Paving the way for the training and retraining of workers, ultimately reducing the costs of production.

Managers are expected to carry out certain basic functions such as
- planning,
- organizing,
- supervising,
- directing,
- controlling,
- coordinating,

- delegating,
- motivating and
- carrying out periodic assessments and evaluations to ensure that the firm's objectives are being carried out.

In practice every business is answerable to particular stakeholders such as directors, shareholders, customers, employees, the government and society.

ADDITIONAL MANAGEMENT FUNCTIONS

Managers owe it to shareholders and owners to do their utmost to make the highest profit possible and to position the business so that it can attract a sizeable market share. Shareholders and owners expect a proper return on their investment so that one managerial goal is to increase the wealth of shareholders and owners.

MANAGEMENT AND EMPLOYEES

Employees are hired for their productivity and skill and employees expect proper working conditions, opportunities for further training and a proper flow of communication between themselves and management. Where communication breaks down and employees are dissatisfied they may resort to malingering, sick outs, work to rule and even strike action. Many workers, expecting trouble from Managers join labour unions so as to strengthen their voice and ensure that they have effective representation. Managers should always attempt a smooth flow of communication between themselves and workers and should put grievance procedures in place so that when employees have concerns, they could use the grievance procedure. Most Caribbean governments have established Ministries of Labour, part of whose responsibility is to mediate and conciliate when there are big disputes between workers and their employers.

MANAGERS RESPONSIBILITY TO CUSTOMERS

Customers have their own tastes and preferences and indeed their own way of looking at life.

Managers should ensure that customers can deal with their business by shopping in comfort, by receiving the necessary attention from staff and by such things as the prompt addressing of complaints as well as proper after sales service.

MANAGERS RESPONSIBILITY TO GOVERNMENT

Managers should ensure that all Government rules and regulations are obeyed.

Secondly Managers should make sure that where Government has the right to inspect premises that there are no problems put in the way of Government inspectors. Managers should also observe Government rules on occupational safety and health.

CHARACTERISTICS OF A GOOD LEADER

The characteristics noted below are those of a good leader:

- Must be competent in his job.
- Know how to delegate, when to delegate and to whom to delegate.
- Must have a sense of empathy with his employees and even with customers.
- Should always be willing to accept new responsibility.
- Should be strong and firm without being unnecessarily aggressive and hostile.
- Should be concerned about the development of staff
- Should focus on team building

LEADERSHIP STYLES

There are three basic leadership styles:

- The Democratic type of leader
- The Laissez Faire type of leader
- The Authoritarian type of leader

THE DEMOCRATIC STYLE OF LEADERSHIP

Strengths of the democratic style

The Democratic style leader allows for subordinates to have a say in decision making. This type of leader also feels that personnel at all levels should be allowed to be heard.

Weakness of the Democratic System

Under the democratic system of leadership especially in very large organizations, it is difficult for the final and ultimate manager to reach out to all members of staff. Some subordinates do not have much regard for democratic leaders because they perceive them as weak. Where the practitioners of the democratic style have been in the habit of practicing excessive consultation and have always engaged its staff in decision making, when crises occur at the workplace or there is need for rapid decision making, the democratic leader may not be able to handle an urgent crisis.

LAISSEZ FAIRE

Advantages

The Laissez Faire type of leader takes an optimistic view of human beings by thinking that each person on staff would function in accordance with wisdom. The Laissez Faire leader thinks that grown employees should know their responsibility and so there is no need for close supervision.

Disadvantages

Practical experience shows that Laissez Faire leaders are perceived by their employees as being too inactive.

Secondly, Laissez Faire leaders are often failures when it comes to dealing with indisciplined employees.

Thirdly, like the democratic leader who is not good at handling emergencies the laissez faire leader fails when rapid decisions have to be made or where crises occur.

AUTHORITARIAN LEADER

Advantages

1. The authoritarian leader tends to be a strong person who makes it known that he/she is in charge.
2. The authoritarian leader is quick to detect slackness and malingering and does not hesitate to act in cases of crises or emergency.

The negative side of Authoritarian Leaders

Authoritarian leaders tend to be tyrannical. They tend not to listen to subordinates. Staff is allowed very limited involvement in decision making.

It is important to note, however, that an effective leader knows when to utilize the relevant style of leadership given the particular situation with which he / she is faced

RESEARCH TASKS

1.   Find out what delegation by management really entails.
2.   Carefully research organizational charts and their meanings and importance.
3.   Trace possible causes of conflict in the work place.
4.   Carefully assess the value of teamwork in an organization.
5.   Carefully ascertain the various functions of management.
6.   What does each function entail?

QUESTIONS

1.   (a)   Provide a definition of an authoritarian leader.

      (b)   What is a laissez-faire leadership?

2   Shiv is resented by almost everybody on his staff but always seems to be on top of things. Courtney on the other hand always involves his workers in decision-making but is seen as fairly ineffective.

      Explain the probable reasons why Shiv is seen as a success while Courtney is deemed ineffective.

3.   Identify the stakeholders to whom managers are answerable.
4.   List four characteristics of an effective leader.
5.   Explain the importance of these four characteristics.
6.   What is delegation?

CHAPTER 8

MARKETING

THE MARKET

Historically 'market' was described as a place where sellers and buyers came together to trade and do business. However in this highly technological era of faxes, e-mails and e-commerce it is no longer necessary in every case for sellers and buyers to meet face to face. The situation on the Stock Exchanges is one in which buyers and sellers of stocks and shares do not really see each other but persons acting for them known as brokers arrange sales.

Producers and their marketers use the term 'market' either to refer to a body of purchasers and potential buyers and/ or specific segments or numbers of buyers to be 'targeted' when products are being made available for sale.

MARKETING

According to the Chartered Institute of Marketing, "Marketing is the management process responsible for identifying, anticipating and satisfying customer requirements profitably".

The marketing process therefore includes the following activities:

1.   Market Research.
2.   Pricing.
3.   Packaging and Labelling.
4.   Branding.
5.   Sales Promotion.
6.   Personal selling
7.   Public relations
8.   Customer relations
9.   Advertising.
10.   Distribution including transport.

MARKET RESEARCH

Very often new producers as well as firms involved in business for a long time undertake measures by which they set out to investigate trends and conditions in the market. This process is called market research. One of the objectives of market research is to check for consumer preferences and any criticisms or concerns which consumers and clients have with regard to factors such as:

(a)   Quality of Goods.
(b)   Pricing of Goods.
(c)   Availability of Goods.
(d)   Promptness of Delivery.
(e)   After- sales service.
(f)   The position of competing products in the market.

MARKET SEGMENTATION

Market segmentation is the breakdown of a market into discrete and identifiable elements, each of which may have its own special requirements of a product and each of which is likely to exhibit different habits affecting its exposure to marketing media.

A market segment may be based on age, gender, income, social standing all referred to as demographic factors; geographical location; and leisure pursuits which are referred to as psychographic factors.

CARRYING OUT MARKET RESEARCH

Market research may be either Secondary or Primary. As far as Secondary Research is concerned, information which is already in existence is used.

Existing publications, reviews, magazines, newspaper articles, websites and any official records make up secondary sources of research. In addition critiques done on radio and television are examples of secondary research.

On the other hand primary research involves the collection of entirely new information and consists of interviews, traditional surveys which utilize questionnaires, observation, experimentation, product sampling and focus group surveys.

Research may be deemed to be quantitative or qualitative. Quantitative research refers to the collection of data which is subject to statistical analysis. This type of research utilizes surveys, random samples, and coded questions which can provide specific answers. Qualitative research unearths customers' motivations, attitudes and behaviours. This research is usually undertaken in small groups of about eight to twelve of a particular market segment which are called focus groups. The size of the group does not allow for reliable statistical analysis.

Although entirely new firms often undertake market research, some businesses which have been producing for varying lengths of time conduct market research to ascertain market conditions so as to be able to better position themselves and to compete more aggressively in the market.

PRICING

Pricing which is concerned with setting what monetary charge(s) consumers will be called on to pay is an important marketing activity.

The price set by the producer depends on the strategy which is being pursued. Pricing may be determined by the following strategies:

- Price skimming which involves charging a high initial price especially for specialty products
- Penetration pricing which entails charging a low price to gain market share quickly
- Competitor-based pricing which involves matching prices with competitors'
- Demand- based or perceived value pricing which is related to the firm's perception of the price the market will find acceptable
- Cost plus pricing, a situation in which the firm adds a percentage to the unit cost per item
- Predatory pricing where the firm undercuts competitors to force them out of the market
- Price discrimination which involves charging different prices in different markets for the same item
- Loss leader pricing, a situation in which a product is sold below cost to generate orders for other products in the same market
- Psychological pricing which focuses on the consumer's perception of value associated with price

PACKAGING AND LABELLING

Here the size, colour, shape, container and label of the product come into focus. Where the package and with it the label proves attractive to consumers, the product will have a special appeal. Labels normally identify the product or brand, the grade of the product, its origin, and any special characteristics.

The package and label will give the product its own identity.

BRANDING

Branding is concerned with naming the product, portraying its colour scheme, and presenting its logo.

SALES PROMOTION

Promoting products can take many different forms, the objective being not simply to inform the buying public about the presence of products in the market place but also by stimulating interest in what is being made available for sale.

Sales promotion refers to measures, often short-term ones, designed to influence wholesalers, retailers and consumers to purchase particular products. The ultimate aim of sales promotion activity is to maximize sales by means of a number of strategies. Empirical observation has shown that the typical sales promotion strategy is either a one-off or periodic event.

Sales promotion activities include competitions, discounts, displays and exhibitions.

PERSONAL SELLING

Personal selling involves the use of salespersons to make direct contact with potential customers in order to persuade those customers to purchase a firm's products and services.

Some firms because of the rules relating to the particular profession are not allowed to advertise and therefore utilize personal selling methods to attract clients.

The process of personal selling includes acquiring knowledge of the product for sale and prospecting for clients through various means such as directories, club memberships, personal contact with centres of influence, friends and acquaintances, and cold canvass methods (making unannounced calls on businesses or persons) in the initial stage. Before approaching the potential clients the sales person will prepare an appropriate presentation which observes the AIDA principle. This principle states that the salesperson should attract Attention through various methods such as display of promotional materials, creating Interest through discerning the tastes of the consumer and developing a Desire for the product from the customer through emotional appeals which may lead to Action. Action is usually in the form of money paid or some tangible commitment to paying for the item.

Salespersons may be paid a combination of fixed income and commission or simply commission. Managers of sales departments may be motivated to drive sales through being rewarded with departmental commissions based on the overall sales of the department.

PUBLIC RELATIONS

Public relations is planned and sustained effort to establish goodwill and mutual understanding between and organization and its publics. Publics refer to employees, management, shareholders, investors, news media, government officials, suppliers, opinion formers, local communities and customers.

As a marketing activity public relations lends to a favourable environment in which to conduct business. It includes matters such as showing respect to all your publics. The firm may use various media to transmit its message of good will. These include electronic and print media as well as social media. It may also sponsor events as a form of goodwill towards a particular audience.

CUSTOMER RELATIONS

Customer relations is really a subset of public relations but firms prioritize customer relations because of the potential for great negative impact when positive customer relations is absent. Staff members are usually trained in the delivery of customer service excellence. The essence of customer relations is the creation of 'good feelings' among customers. The need for reliability, credibility, attractiveness, responsiveness, and empathy are all emphasized.

ADVERTISING

Advertising is a very important activity in free enterprise and mixed economic systems. The reason for this statement is the presence of competition in the market in these two economic systems.

At its most basic and primary level, the purpose of advertising is to make known the presence and availability of goods and services.

FORMS OF ADVERTISING

Advertising may either be direct or indirect.   With direct advertising, marketers target segments of market or the market as a whole and try to reach their 'targets' directly by seeking out and 'going' straight to those at whom the advertising is aimed.

Where letters, posters, fliers and circulars as well as catalogues are delivered direct and straight to those for whom they are intended, direct advertising is realised.

Indirect advertising on the other hand is 'advertising to the public at large'.

BENEFITS OF ADVERTISING

1.   It provides information to consumers.
2.   It stimulates demand.
3.   It can therefore cause sales to be increased.

THE NEGATIVE SIDE OF ADVERTISING

- Advertising can cause people to buy items and services which they really do not need.
- Advertising is usually very expensive.
- The final prices of goods and services are increased to reflect the cost of advertising so the consumer ends up contributing to the cost of advertising.

TYPES OF ADVERTISING

As far as the nature of advertising is concerned there are four types of advertising namely:

Informative Advertising
Persuasive Advertising
Competitive Advertising
Generic Advertising

INFORMATIVE ADVERTISING

This type of advertising:

(a)   Makes the consumer aware of the availability of products and services, including any noteworthy features of what is being offered for sale.

(b)   Merely outlines to customers where the products can be obtained.

(c)   Indicates the price of the product.

(d)   Indicates if after sales service is available.

(e)   Offers instructions as to how the product(s) are to be used.

PERSUASIVE ADVERTISING

Here the emphasis is on wooing or enticing the consumer to buy goods and services.

Presentation of such advertisements is characterized by pointed language, stories and in some cases powerful visual messages.

COMPETITIVE ADVERTISING

This type of advertising is sometimes known as Comparison advertising. It is designed to lure consumers away from competitors by assertions that the advertised product is the best kind and has superiority over rival and competing products and services.

GENERIC ADVERTISING

"USE MORE CHOCOLATE".

"Red wine is good for the heart"

The two examples above focus attention on using a kind or kinds of products without recommending any specific brand by name. Professional persons and those with an interest in the community are the people who will likely recommend a 'genus' or generalized product more so than a given brand. This kind of advertising may also be used to promote an industry, sector or generic product.

THE MARKETING MIX

The main elements of marketing which can be varied to meet consumers' needs effectively are referred to as the marketing mix. The marketing mix has traditionally comprised four P's which include:

(a) Product
(b) Price
(c) Place
(d) Promotion

In more recent times three (3) more P's have been added. These are:
- People
- Physical evidence
- Process

PRODUCT

The marketer must ensure that the product is of the right quality and that it carries features which would lure the consumer to it.

The product is determined by such factors as quality, size, presentation, design, packaging, and taste.

PRICE

The firm makes decisions about the price of the product being offered. Among issues of price which the firm may consider are determinations of list price, discount price, special price, and competitive price. Different markets may require different pricing structures as indicated in an earlier section on price.

PLACE

Place refers to the location of the firm as well as the method of distribution to make the product accessible to the consumer. Consideration has to be given to specific location to facilitate access of a large target audience in some cases. For this reason some businesses are established in town centres instead of rural areas.

The distribution of the product by modern internet media, by traditional means like motorized or non-motorised vehicles, air and sea craft, rail, or salespersons on foot all merit consideration as appropriate.

PROMOTION

The fundamental purpose of promotion is to bring the consumer's attention to the availability of products in the market.

Promotion can take many forms including:

(a) Personal Selling.
(b) Advertising.
(c) Exhibitions and Trade shows.
(d) Special bargains and discounts.
(e) Public Relations strategies.

PEOPLE

The relevance of people in the marketing mix stems from the fact that customer agents, sales personnel and management can highly influence the success of the marketing effort. The firm therefore has to take great care with the selection of these persons.

PHYSICAL EVIDENCE

Physical evidence refers to the ambience, colour scheme, use of logos, seating arrangement and quality of furniture and décor and other amenities which add to the attractiveness of the business.

PROCESS

Process refers to the speed and ease with which products and service are delivered and the manner in which any consumer challenges are handled.

SITUATIONAL ANALYSIS

Before making a decision on the marketing activities to be pursued a firm should assess its capability in the market place through undertaking a SWOT analysis. This examines the present situation of the firm. The areas to consider include the following:

- Strengths which entail its marketing capacity including its brand, distribution, location, cash flow position, profitability, capital base, management, staff, and operations.
- Weaknesses which include the points noted for strengths since the firm may be strong in some of these areas and weak in others.
- Opportunities which could include its flexibility to enter a complimentary market or to diversify in the same industry.
- Threats which include the impact of change in legislation, competition from new entrants to the market, declining markets, new technology replacing existing technology.

An examination of the macro-economic environment is also essential. This requires what is known as a PEST Analysis. In more recent times this has been extended to the STEEPLE analysis. The PEST Analysis includes consideration of such factors as:

- Political which refers to the impact of laws and governmental decisions, rules and regulations
- Economic which refers to the influence of standard of living, cost of living, exchange rates, interest rates, competition among firms, and similar economic variables.
- Social factors which relate to cultural trends and behaviours, lifestyles, religion, values etc
- Technological which is concerned with the firm's use of technology for production, distribution and sales

The STEEPLE model has extended this analysis to single out specific areas. These include Social, Technological, Economic, Environmental, Political, Legal and Ethical factors.

THE MARKETING STRATEGIES

There are a number of options for strategies which the firm may consider. These include the following:

- market penetration
- market development
- new product development
- differentiation
- cost leadership
- niche marketing
- mass marketing

A marketing penetration strategy may be used for a current product in an existing market. The strategy involves trying to attract a greater share of the market through reducing prices and increasing promotion.

A market development strategy is used when a firm is launching a product in a new market. It entails examining the conditions which exist in that market. A PEST or STEEPLE Analysis should be used. This would be particularly necessary if the firm is entering an overseas market. For example if a Barbadian firm wishes to start trading in St. Lucia a market development strategy should be employed.

A new product development strategy should be used if the firm is developing a new product for an existing market. This would entail undertaking research into the possibilities for the new product such as its ingredients, packaging, branding, labelling and pricing. This process also involves undertaking feasibility studies, testing for safety and quality, test marketing (sampling and experimentation) before the product is finally launched.

Differentiation is used as a strategy when the firm produces a product which is perceived to have more benefits than other competing brands. This is usually the case when a firm can develop a brand which is seen as superior and thus can attract a higher price.

A Cost Leadership strategy thrives on the containment of input cost. Usually firms which buy inputs in bulk can get them at a much cheaper price and therefore can pass on the gains in the form of lower prices for the product.

Niche marketing involves using strategies directed at a small segment of a larger market. For example a producer of special fashion design may select a niche market and utilize a strategy which allows that producer to access that market. This may require obtaining referrals from existing clients.

A Mass Marketing strategy is targeted at a large market in terms of sales volume. The products being promoted are usually consumable items such as bread, biscuits, beverages, soaps, sugar, flour etc. The use of a wide range of media is usually required.

MARKETING OBJECTIVES

Marketing objectives are quantifiable targets which the firm sets itself. These objectives should be
- **S**pecific
- **M**easurable
- **A**ttainable
- **R**ealistic and
- **T**ime-based

Objectives are usually related to items such as sales, market share, and brand awareness. For example a firm may have the following as its objectives:

- To increase sales by 10 % by the end of the year
- To increase market share by 20 % by the end of the year

THE MARKETING PLAN

The Marketing Plan may be outlined as follows:
- Situational analysis comprising information on the product, the SWOT and PEST Analysis.
- The marketing objectives (as indicated above)
- Product features and pricing

- The target markets which will include main markets and market segments
- The marketing strategy (as indicated above)
- The Marketing Activities which will include proposed promotional methods.
- The Marketing Budget

MARKETING AUDIT

A marketing audit is a comprehensive, systematic, independent, and periodic examination of a firm's marketing environment, objectives, strategies, and activities with a view to determining problem areas and opportunities and recommending a plan of action to improve the firm's marketing performance.

To facilitate review of the effectiveness of the marketing strategies a Marketing Audit is recommended.

RESEARCH TASKS

1. Carefully explore the concept of mass production.
2. How does the 'market approach' to pricing compare with the cost approach to marketing?
3. Critically assess and evaluate the importance of the four traditional P's.
4. Why is market research important?
5. Is it true that much money is wasted on advertising? How is this so?
6. Provide examples of niche markets.

QUESTIONS

1. Explain with examples what is meant by market research
2. Why would a firm trading for close to twenty years commission market research.
3. Why would a completely new business be advised to conduct market research.
4. Carefully identify and assess the importance of

    (a)   Packaging and Labelling;
    (b)   Branding; and
    (c)   Sales Promotion.
5. Suggest three negative features of advertising.
6. Advise advertisers as to how they should go about carrying out their tasks as advertisers.

CHAPTER 9

DISTRIBUTION AND SELLING

The traditional Chain of Distribution starts from the Producer and travels along a distribution chain via the Wholesaler to the Retailer and then to the final Consumer.

In recent years it has occurred that some producers and manufacturers find ways to sell direct to consumers while others sell direct to retailers.

THE MANUFACTURER AND PRODUCER

The producer is the firm or entity that 'makes' or supervises production. Producers of eggs, tomatoes, sweet potatoes and garlic among other things do produce and or supervise production (at the primary stage of production).

A challenge faced by manufacturers is by what means his/her goods can best get to the market and so a decision must be taken as to whether to use the services of a wholesaler or if to locate a retailer or if to sell direct to the final consumers. In some instances the first firm which buys from the manufacturer may not be the very final consumer but may be some other business person who buys for further conversion and processing thereby adding value to what the original manufacturer has produced.

In following the traditional chain of distribution consideration will now be given to the wholesaler.

THE WHOLESALER

The wholesaler is a middleman who buys from producers and sells to retailers and in some cases to final consumers.

Other functions of the wholesaler include the following:

- Importing goods which are not produced locally.
- Purchasing in large volumes from various sources and building up inventories.
- Providing information to producers on market conditions in the locality where goods are to be traded.
- Advising retailers about the availability of various commodities.
- Offering credit and discounts to retailers.
- Offering transportation to retailers.
- Marketing available varieties of products in local markets.
- Packaging and assembling goods on behalf of some producers.

CHALLENGES FACING MODERN WHOLESALERS

- Some producers deal directly with retailers thereby bypassing the wholesaler.
- On occasions the wholesaler's stock and inventory build up to unacceptably high levels
- There may be perishable goods in stock which may spoil before being sold.
- Some retailers have their own storage facilities which permit them to bypass the wholesaler and deal directly with producers.

THE RETAILER

The retailer is usually the entity which sells to the final consumer.

As far as retailing functions are concerned retailers make products available in manageable quantities. Retailers tend to sell small quantities.

Retailers often either locate very close to market or use various transportation methods to access the local market.

Some retailers offer advice to final consumers about goods before purchases are made.

Retailers provide after- sales service to final consumers. Some retailers also offer credit to their customers.

TYPES OF RETAILERS

Retailers include the following:

Hawkers, Higglers and Hucksters
Small sole proprietorship village shops
Mini – Marts or Superettes
Supermarkets
Hyper Markets
Convenience Stores
Discount Stores
Department Stores
Vending Machines

GENERAL TRANSPORT

Transport is concerned with the movement of products and people and is an important facilitator of commerce and trade.

Transport is necessary to move:-

(i)   Goods from the producer to the wholesaler.
(ii)   Goods from the wholesaler to the retailer.
(iii) Goods from the retailer to the final consumer.
(iv)   Raw materials and factor inputs from their source to producers.
(v)   Workers to their places of work.
(vi)   Tourists from abroad.
(vii) Tourists who need to attend conferences, sporting events and places of interest.

TYPES OF TRANSPORT

Products may be transported through the following means:

1. Rail (Train)
2. Road
3. Pipelines
4. Containers
5. By sea and water

Rail

There are but few railways in the Caribbean and so trains are hardly in use.

Bauxite which is an important industry in Guyana and Jamaica has been transported by rail for years but in most Caribbean countries trains are not in use. Transportation by railway is not a major activity in the English-speaking Caribbean but where it is in use it is good for very long distances and can carry bulky goods like bauxite.

Road

Transport by road is definitely the most common means of moving products and people in the English-speaking Caribbean.

Road transport is flexible and can reach almost every destination in a given country. As far as transporting goods is concerned road transport can consist of moderately sized delivery vans right down to ordinary trucks and specially adapted vehicles, such as refrigerated trucks.

The choice of a specific means of road transport depends on the size and types of product to be used for safety and to prevent the loss of goods.

When the relatively small size of Caribbean territories is taken into account, then it will be understood that in internal trade, transport by road is in considerable use.

Pipelines

Pipelines are in use to transport water, gas and oil.

Pipelines carry products to final destination often by the linking and attachment to smaller, shorter pipes.

In view of the character of water, gas and oil, pipelines prove convenient to those who make use of what they transport.

Problems can be encountered as far as the capital costs associated with installing entirely new pipelines and there is often the problem of some pipelines being broken.

Maintaining pipelines incurs costs and there is inconvenience to consumers when burst pipelines prevent the efficient delivery of products.

Containers

Large trailers made of metal and often designed and built to standard sizes are in use and are known as containers. These are special huge boxes.

When products are stored and transported in containers the costs of handling products are kept down. This is so since the need for manual labour and its costs are minimised.

The ships and trucks which transport these containers tend to have a speedier turnaround time. Containers can be costly. However, because they can be carefully sealed, the incidence of pilferage can be reduced.

Containers come in various sizes and can be hoisted on to trucks for transport to final destination.

By sea and water

Large ocean-going cargo ships can transport huge amounts of products at relatively cheap costs.

Most cargo ships are reliable and bring substantial amounts of goods to Caribbean countries.

At a time since virtually every Caribbean country has a viable tourism sector, cruise ship and passenger ships serve to transport tourists to Caribbean territories.

What is referred to above deals with vessels which travel on the seas. However, Belize has been known to float logs of wood down rivers to particular destinations. The use of rivers therefore features in commerce and trade.

The above represents the chief means of moving products and people but the choice of the specific means of transport depends on:

(a)   Quantities to be transported.
(b)   Speed of delivery.
(c)   Costs.
(d)   Safety in transport.

RESEARCH TASKS

Transport has been identified as a facilitator of commerce, business and trade. Explain other areas of activity which also facilitate commerce, business and trade.

QUESTIONS

1. What is the chain of distribution? Provide examples in support of your answer.
2. Henry a retired businessman has advised his friend Harry to leave out his wholesaler. Harry is thinking about it and asks you to provide three reasons why Henry has taken the position he has. Advise Harry.
3. Give three reasons why some consumers go straight to warehouses and wholesalers' outlets to do business.
4. Using four facts make out a case why wholesalers ought not to be eliminated from the chain of distribution.
6.   Provide three reasons why transport is important in:
    (a)   Foreign Trade.
    (b)   The local, domestic trade.

CHAPTER 10

HUMAN RESOURCE MANAGEMENT

Human resource management is the utilization of human resources to achieve organizational goals.

This involves attracting the right number of employees with the required knowledge , skills, and attitudes; developing employees to face the challenges in their jobs; providing a safe environment; facilitating harmonious relationships among all levels of staff; maintaining systems for motivating staff; and planning to provide the necessary manpower for the organization.

In effect human resource management includes the following activities:
- Recruitment
- Selection
- Training
- Industrial Relations
- Compensation
- Health and safety
- Manpower planning

RECRUITMENT

Recruitment is the process of attracting suitable personnel to fill the vacancies in an organization. The process involves job analysis, job evaluation, job description, person specification, and communication.

Job analysis entails examining the elements of a job such as its tasks, responsibilities, duties etc. Job evaluation assesses the relative worth of a job to ensure that the rewards for one job are fair compared to others in the organization. Job description refers to a statement detailing information on the job available. This information includes job title, duties, tasks, and reporting relationships. The person specification defines the requirements for the potential job holder. These requirements include age, qualifications, experience, skills, and special circumstances such as ability to drive.

Communicating the message of the job availability is executed through such means as internal job postings; referrals via existing staff members to persons outside the organization; contacting schools, colleges, and universities; liaising with employment agencies; recruiting from other firms; appropriate advertising in various print and electronic media including social media. The business may also undertake job fairs which serve to attract a large number of applicants in a short period of time. Internships or apprenticeships also provide an opportunity to attract persons to the organization.

Usually the business will require the applicant to submit a curriculum vitae which details the applicants' educational achievements, experience, skills, and other relevant personal information. It is usually presented in chronological order starting from most recent details. The firm may also require the applicants to fill out a standard application form so that comparison of candidates may be easily discernible.

SELECTION

Selection refers to the process of choosing the most appropriate candidate for the job. The process usually begins with a preliminary short -listing of applicants based on the job description and the person specification and how the applicants' personal information matches with the requirements.

Persons selected at this stage undergo a preliminary interview. They may also be subjected to various tests such as cognitive tests and job knowledge tests. Arising from this stage of the process the list of applicants is shortened and those selected may be interviewed in greater detail to determine their suitability in terms of experience, education and training, attitude, deportment, and organizational fit. Background checks are usually made on the ones deemed to be most suitable for the job before a final decision is made. The selected persons usually have to undergo physical examination or other similar test like drug tests before being formally offered a position with the business.

In special cases selection tests may also include psychomotor tests which seek to measure strength, coordination and dexterity; personality tests which are used to classify personality types; work sample tests which require an applicant to perform a task or set of tasks representative of the job.

TRAINING AND DEVELOPMENT

Training refers to activities designed to provide workers with the knowledge, skill, and attitude required for their present job while development includes learning that looks beyond the requirements of the present job and is more concerned with career building.

The training and development process starts with a recognition of a need for change and then a determination of the deficits identified. The business will then establish specific objectives and select the relevant training methods and media which will then be followed with the implementation of the relevant programmes. An evaluation of the programmes will then follow.

Some of the training and development methods which may be used include the following:
- Coaching

- Mentoring
- Business games
- Role playing
- Behaviour modelling
- Class room instruction
- Vestibule training
- Simulation

Coaching involves one-on-one training conducted by a manager or supervisor on an ongoing basis.

Mentoring is also an on-the-job approach in which the trainee learns from more experienced staff on an ongoing basis with a view to building a career.

Business games are simulations which represent actual business situations. The participants are assigned various organizational roles and they are nurtured in the skills of making decisions relating to the respective roles chosen.

Role playing, a limited version of business games, requires participants to respond to specific problems they may encounter in their jobs. This is suitable method for training in customer care.

Behaviour modelling seeks to demonstrate the correct ways of handling various work situations. Videotapes and DVDs are used for this purpose.

Class room instruction uses traditional methods of teaching including lectures, discussion and practical sessions to communicate knowledge and skills to trainees.

Vestibule training allows for training on equipment which closely resembles that used on the job. Training is usually done off-site.

Simulation involves the use of devices which duplicate real world situations. Many of these devices are computerized. Aircraft simulators are prime examples of the necessity to use this method.

Training programmes should be evaluated to determine the extent to which objectives were achieved. Some of the methods used include obtaining participants' opinions through issuing evaluation forms. Tests may also be given to the participants to see what they have learnt. Observation of behavioural change may also be recorded overtime.

INDUSTRIAL RELATIONS

Industrial relations also referred to as employer: employee relations and labour relations refers to the processes and practices for maintaining excellent relations between the employer and employees.

In the relationship with their employers employees expect fair wages and salaries, opportunities for advancement, provision of suitable and safe conditions of work, suitable training opportunities, appropriate means to resolve disputes and grievances, effective means of communication, consultation and negotiation procedures.

On the other hand, employers expect the employees to provide effective and efficient work, commitment to the business and its objectives, loyalty, acceptance of the business' codes of conduct, willingness to undertake any work reasonably asked of them and cooperation.

One of the means through which communication may be facilitated is the establishment of Work Councils and Committees which can make inputs into the running of the business. Some businesses have Staff Associations which represent the interest of the employees. They function like trade unions except that their action can only impact on the business at which they work.

Trade Unions represent a body of workers from several businesses. These unions may be general unions which represent a cross-section of businesses. There are also craft unions which represent employees with a particular skill; industrial unions which are set up for employees in different industries like the petroleum industry; and white collar unions which represent employees in professional services such as teachers.

Unions are usually involved in the following activities:
- Negotiation for salaries and wages
- Grievance procedure
- Consultation on conditions of work

Apart from these activities some unions also assist members by providing training, low cost housing and insurance, and credit union services.

The union takes industrial action when a grievance has not been addressed satisfactorily by the employer. Industrial action may take the following forms:
- Go slow
- Work to rule
- Overtime bans
- Sick outs
- Strikes

Grievance procedure is a formal, systematic process which allows employees to resolve complaints of alleged or real breaches of the terms and conditions of their employment. Grievances should be settled as promptly as possible. The usual procedure starts with the handling of the problem at the level where it originated. In effect, if a worker has a problem at the stage of the supervisor the worker will not run directly to the Manager. An attempt should be made to resolve the problem with the supervisor. If attempts to resolve the problem fail the matter should then be raised at a higher level and the assistance of the union or Staff Association representative should be sought. As matters remain unresolved discussion would proceed to high levels in the organization with union representatives from the Union itself being called in.

The employer may also call their employers' organization to represent them. If matters remain unresolved Government Agencies such as the Labour department may be required to intervene, bringing representatives of workers and the employer together to resolve the subject of the grievance.

COMPENSATION

The human resource management function involves compensating staff appropriately. The business may compensate staff based on industry standards, the experience of the staff member, the ability of the business to pay, the law as determined by the legal MinimumWage for particular types of work, and bargaining agreements with unions.

The business has several options for compensation. These include fixed wages and salaries; commissions; payment for piece work; share option schemes; profit sharing; fringe benefits including cheap loans, subsidized food and accommodation, health care, preferential access to the business' products or services, company discounts; and annual bonuses.

HEALTH AND SAFETY

The business has to ensure that there is compliance with Government rules and regulations pertaining to health and safety in the work place.

The employer should provide a safe working environment and relevant safety equipment, clothing and training.

The Human Resources Department has a responsibility to also ensure that employees are guided by the safety regulations and rules of the business, Government Agencies and Departments.

MANPOWER PLANNING

The human resource function requires that the business adjusts its manpower needs to meet the objectives of the organization. On some occasion the business may anticipate that redundancies may be necessary in the medium term and would have to plan its execution of the redundancy programme to minimize any fallouts arising therefrom.

RESEARCH TASKS

1. Check a medium-sized company to find out the kind of staff training programmes it conducts.

2. Visit a trade union and discuss with its officers the nature of their activities.

3. Observe the kinds of recruitment advertisements which are placed in the mass media.

4. Research Performance Appraisal

QUESTIONS

1. Explain the process of recruitment and selection.

2. Describe five different methods of compensation

3. Explain the purpose of manpower planning

CHAPTER 11

SOURCES OF FINANCE

A business will need finance from its inception and on an ongoing basis. Initially it will usually need equipment and machinery and the provision of working capital will be critical.

The working capital includes the day to day finance available for recurrent expenditure such as labour costs; rent; purchases of raw materials and components; and cash.

The main sources of finance in the early stages if the business is a sole trader or partnership will be the owners' savings or any funds that they can attract from relatives, friends, and well-wishers.

One of the ways of riding through a difficult cash flow situation in the early stages of the business is through accessing trade credit. This refers to a facility where items can be bought and paid for usually thirty (30) days later, thus allowing the business to sell the items and then pay for them.

The business may also conserve on the outflow of cash by using a hire purchase system to obtain some equipment and machinery. This arrangement allows the business to make a downpayment and then pay for the items on a monthly basis over a specified period of time. Leasing may also be considered. For vehicles this may be suitable since this avoids a large initial outflow as payments are paid monthly on a rental basis.

Businesses may also negotiate to obtain an overdraft to protect themselves against the vagaries of cash flow situations such as depletion of cash which may be required to pay for such monthly commitments as rent and labour wages. The overdraft allows the business to pay its bills even if the business' bank account does not have enough money to cover cheques being used. Interest is paid when the bank account is overdrawn up to an agreed limit.

For some assets such as a vehicle or a piece of equipment the firm may require a bank loan which is repaid over a fixed period of time at regular intervals, usually every month. Interest is added to the money loaned.

It is desirable that profits be ploughed back into the business as a viable source of finance without the stringencies of other sources like loans.

Private and public limited companies may obtain funds through issuing shares of which there are two types, ordinary shares and preference shares. For ordinary shares shareholders receive a dividend when the business makes a profit and declares a dividend. For preference shares a fixed dividend is offered but the shareholder has no voting rights. The business would have created a liability when it offered the preferred share. Businesses therefore usually offer ordinary shares.

As the business grows it may decide to access a mortgage for new buildings using the buildings as collateral. A mortgage is a long term loan which is protected by collateral. Overtime the accrued interests make a mortgage an expensive undertaking even though it is being repaid in monthly installments.

Some businesses in high risks ventures may benefit from funds contributed by venture capitalists who input loan capital as well as share capital. The venture capitalists therefore have a great measure of control over the running of the business as major shareholders.

Some governments also offer grants to businesses in some developmental areas. However, business plans have to be submitted in order to obtain grants. Special conditions are also applied, for example the business may have to indicate that over a specified time it was making progress with its business venture. The grants are usually provided over a period of time in various tranches subject to reports on the various phases of the chosen project.

RESEARCH TASKS

1. Check the leasing arrangements for a vehicle at any automobile dealer.

2. Research the activities of a venture capitalist.

3. Research the terms of a mortgage arrangement.

4. Thoroughly research 'joint venture'.

QUESTIONS

1. Describe three sources of finance for a sole trader

2. Describe two other sources of finance which can be a applied to a private limited company

3. Compare and contrast 'shares' in credit unions with 'shares' in limited liability companies.

CHAPTER 12

BUSINESS ACCOUNTING

Accounting is concerned with the collection of data of a firm's activities which is presented in monetary terms in suitable forms to facilitate decision making.

Users of accounting information include managers, supervisors, employees and Boards of Directors. External users include potential investors, lenders, suppliers, and relevant government departments.

The principal accounting documents for final accounts are:

- The Balance sheet
- Profit and Loss statement;

Other documents which are used by the firm on an ongoing basis include the following:

- Bank reconciliation statement
- Cash Flow Forecast

THE BALANCE SHEET

The Balance Sheet is an accounting statement which values, at one point in time, an organisation's assets and liabilities i.e what the organization owns and how this has been financed as at the particular date.

The Balance Sheet lists Fixed Assets, Current Assets, Current Liabilities and Long term Liabilities.

Fixed assets provide a benefit for more than twelve (12) months and can be tangible, intangible or financial. Tangible assets include buildings, factories, vehicles and equipment. Intangible assets include brand name, goodwill and patents; and financial assets are investments in other firms.

Current assets provide a benefit for less than twelve (12) months and include stock, debtors (accounts receivable) and cash. Stock refers to raw materials, work in progress, and finished goods. Debtors include the amount owed to the firm and any prepayments made to another entity. Cash refers to money on hand or money in a financial institution.

Current liabilities include creditors (accounts payable) i.e. money owed for less than a year (12 months), bank overdrafts, taxes and dividends due.

Long term liabilities refer to creditors (accounts payable) i.e. money owed for more than a year. These include loans and mortgages.

The balance sheet presents what the firm owns in terms of its fixed assets and current assets. The sources of finance used to acquire the assets are represented by its current and long term liabilities in addition to its reserves (money earned over a period of time as retained profit) and its equity which is represented by issued shares or owner's funds.

The balance sheet equation equalizes total assets with total liabilities and shareholders (or owner's funds). Please see example of Balance Sheet at Fig 12.1.

PROFIT AND LOSS STATEMENT

The Profit and Loss Statement records all of a firm's revenues, costs and profits or losses made over a specific trading period.

Revenue also referred to as turnover, measures the value of the sales in cash and money owed for the produce of the firm.

Costs include the value of items utilized in the production process which is presented in the Statement as 'cost of sales'; and expenses for overheads which include administrative, utility and general marketing costs.

The Profit and Loss Statement records Gross Profit {profit after the cost of sales has been deducted from Sales (turnover)} and Net Profit (usually presented as Profit after tax or 'Profit attributable to shareholders')

Operating profit is the term used for Gross Profit minus Expenses for administration and general marketing (usually referred to as overheads)

The firm may also benefit from non-operating income which refers to dividends from shares in other companies or interest from financial instruments such as bonds.

A record may also be made of 'Profit before interest and tax' to reflect the fact that at this point the firm may still be liable for interest payable on loans. The Statement will therefore indicate the Profit on ordinary activities before tax on profits after interest costs have been deducted.

Profit after tax will then be recorded after corporation tax has been deducted. Dividends paid to shareholders will then be deducted to arrive at Retained Profit. Please see example of Profit and Loss Statement at Fig 12.2

BANK RECONCILIATION

Bank reconciliation involves the analysis and adjustment of differences in the cash balance shown on the bank statement and the amount shown in the account holder's records. This matching process involves making allowances for cheques issued but not yet presented and for cheques deposited but not yet cleared or credited. Bank charges should also be noted. See example of Bank Reconciliation below at Fig 12.3

CASH FLOW FORECAST

Cash Flow Forecast is a recorded estimate of the timing and amount of cash inflows and outflows over a specific period of time. It indicates the periods when cash will be used up thus requiring the firm to borrow or to use up reserves which are being held. It also shows the periods when cash inflows are expected. See an example below at Fig 12.4:

Cash inflows usually arise from immediate cash sales or from cash being paid on previous credit sales as indicated above. Dividend payments to the business, sale of assets, and interest earned may also be included in cash inflows.

Cash outflows reflect cash expected to leave the business to pay for such items as payments for labour, materials, and rent. Loan repayments, prepayments on bills, interest expenses, taxes and dividend payments may also be included in cash outflows.

The due dates for scheduled payments such as rents, mortgage payments, and loans have to be observed to inform the firm when extra effort has to be made to collect monies owed to the firm or particular drives have to be made to attract increased sales.

Cash flow forecasts may be inaccurate when sales forecast are overestimated due to changing economic circumstances which either increase or decrease demand for goods and services. Customers may be slow to pay because of some unexpected circumstance. Cash outflows may increase because of unanticipated rise in cost of inputs.

Fig 12.1

ABC CO LTD

Balance Sheet as at December 31, 2015

			$ 000
Fixed Assets			**300**
Property	150		
Machinery	50		
Vehicles	100		
Current Assets			**60**
Cash	30		
Stock	20		
Debtors	10		
Less Current Liabilities			**(20)**
Creditors	10		
Short term loans	10		
Net Current Assets			**40**
Assets Employed			**340**
Financed by:			
Issued Share Capital @ $ 1 per share		150	
Reserves		100	
Long term liabilities		90	
CAPITAL EMPLOYED			**340**

Fig 12.2

ABC CO LTD

Profit and Loss Statement

For the year ending December 31, 2015

	$ 000
Sales turnover	300
Cost of Sales	(200)
Gross Profit	**100**
Overheads	80
Operating (Net) Profit	**20**
Interest payable	(5)
Pretax profits	**15**
Tax @ 20 %	(3)
Profit after tax	**12**
Dividends	8
Retained Profit	**4**

Fig. 12. 3
XYZ CO LTD
BANK RECONCILIATION

	$
Opening Cash Account Balance - *[insert date]*	**500,000.00**
Add: Receipts	25,000.00
Less: Payments	80,000.00
Closing Cash Balance - *[insert date]*	**445,000.00 A**
Closing Balance of Bank Account - *[insert date]* **(as per bank statement)**	**460,000.00**
Add: Receipts not banked (refer detailed listing below)	25,000.00
Less: Cheques written but not presented (refer detailed listing below)	40,000.00
	445,000.00 B
Difference (A-B)	0.00

List of Receipts not Banked as at *[insert date]*

Item	Amount	Date banked
	15,000.00	
	10,000.00	
Total	**25,000.00**	

List of Cheques not Presented at *[insert date]*

Payee	Chq. No.	Amount	Date presented
	123	10,000.00	
	124	6,000.00	
	125	12,000.00	
	126	8,000.00	
	127	4,000.00	
	Total	**40,000.00**	

Fig 12.4
A Simple Cash Flow Forecast

ABC CO LTD CASH FLOW FORECAST For period January – April 2016				
$	January	February	March	April
Opening Balance	10000	4000	1000	(500)
Cash in				
Cash sales	4000	6000	8000	10000
Credit sales	-	1000	2500	3500
Cash out				
Materials	6000	6000	8000	10000
Wages	3000	3000	3000	3000
Rent	1000	1000	1000	1000
Closing Balance	4000	1000	(500)	(1000)

RATIO ANALYSIS

Published accounts by themselves do not always indicate the level of performance of a firm.

To facilitate a comparison of one firm with another or with one sector to another or with one year to another it becomes necessary to use a value which makes comparison easier. The use of ratios is therefore a very efficient means of making comparisons although consideration must be given to other relevant factors before making a judgement.

Accountants make comparisons by relating two accounting results to each other to form a ratio. The two most widely used ratios are the liquidity ratio and the profitability ratio

Liquidity ratios

The liquidity ratio determines the extent to which a firm can cover its short-term debts.
Of the two liquidity ratios, the current ratio compares current assets with current liabilities. The equation is as follows:

$$\text{Current ratio} = \frac{\text{Current assets}}{\text{current liabilities}}$$

For example if a firm has current assets of $ 600,000 and current liabilities of 300, 000 using the equation above the calculation would be expressed as follows:

$$\text{Current ratio} = \frac{600,000}{300,000} \quad \text{which equals 2:1}$$

This result indicates that the firm has twice as many assets as liabilities and should be in a favourable position to handle its indebtedness.

A stricter test of the firm's liquidity is undertaken using the acid test ratio which is also known as the quick ratio. This ratio eliminates the stock from the equation. The equation for this ratio is as follows:

$$\text{Acid test ratio} = \frac{\text{Liquid assets}}{\text{current liabilities}}$$

Liquid assets = current assets-stocks

For example if a firm has current assets of $ 600,000 of which stock contributes $ 300,000, liquid assets will be deemed to be $ 300,000.

$$\text{The Acid test ratio} = \frac{300,000}{300,000} = 1:1$$

Lenders to the firm are more likely to consider the acid test ratio since it may more accurately reflect the level of liquidity of the firm (the ability of the firm to convert assets to cash). Stock may in some cases be difficult to convert to cash in a timely manner or may be the kind of stock which has become obsolete or out of style.

Profitability ratios

Profitability ratios are used to measure the performance of a firm as it relates to generation of profits.

Gross profit margin compares gross profit (profit after cost of sales has been deducted from sales (turnover) with sales (turnover). It is recorded as a percentage. The information to calculate this ratio is collected from the Profit and Loss Statement.

Gross profit margin $= \dfrac{\text{Gross profit}}{\text{sales}} \times 100$

If a firm makes $400, 000 in sales but has a gross profit of $ 100,000 the gross profit margin would be recorded as follows:

Gross profit margin $= \dfrac{100{,}000}{400{,}000} \times 100 = 25\,\%$

Net profit margin presents net profit (profit after overheads and other incidental costs like interest charges have been deducted from gross profit) as a percentage of sales (turnover). The information to arrive at this ratio is contained in the Profit and Loss statement.

The equation is as follows:

Net profit margin $= \dfrac{\text{net profit}}{\text{sales}} \times 100$

If a firm makes $ 400, 000 in sales but has a net profit of $ 40, 000 net profit margin would be recorded as

Net profit margin $= \dfrac{40{,}000}{400{,}000} \times 100 = 10\%$

Return on capital employed compares net profit with the capital which has been invested in the firm. The net profit figure is obtained from the Profit and Loss Statement while the Capital employed is garnered from the Balance Sheet. The Capital employed is usually the sum of the funds borrowed (long term loans) and the owners' equity (shareholders' funds)

Return on capital employed $= \text{Net profit} \times 100$

$$\overline{\text{Capital employed}}$$

If a firm makes $ 40,000 in profit and has employed capital of $ 400,000

The Return on Capital employed $= \dfrac{40,000}{400,000}$ x 100

= 10%

BREAK EVEN ANALYSIS

A firm starts any operation with certain fixed costs which have to be accounted for and which are paid for with the sales of the firm. There will therefore be a phase during which the firm is making no profit. It is good business for a firm to have some idea of the point at which it will start to make a profit. This point is determined by the number of products sold and the price of the products.

Break even analysis is concerned with establishing the point at which the firm stops using financial resources without making a profit and starts to get a return (earn a profit). In essence this analysis will determine the level of output at which total costs equal total revenue. In this text we will consider the equation method to arrive at the break-even point.

The break-even formula is as follows:

$$\frac{\text{Fixed costs}}{\text{Contribution per unit}}$$

Contribution per unit = selling price – variable cost

(Variable costs refer to cost which attach themselves to the production of each individual product e.g. materials, labour , taxes)

If a product is sold for $10 but its variable costs per unit add up to $5 its contribution per unit would be $ 5. If we assume a fixed cost of $ 10,000 made up of overheads, administrative and marketing cost the breakeven point in units using the formula above would be arrived at as follows:

$$\frac{\text{Fixed costs} \quad (10,000)}{\text{Contribution} \quad (5)} = 2000 \text{ units}$$

2000 units must be sold to cover the costs of overheads. At this point the firm now begins to earn a profit.

The firm's ability to make a reasonable profit will now be determined by its physical capacity and available market. In this regard, the Margin of Safety may now be worked out. This is defined as the amount by which possible sales may exceed the breakeven point. If the firm can produce 4000 units with its given capacity and have a big enough market to attract that volume of sales the Margin of safety will be worked out as follows:

Margin of Safety = Capacity-Breakeven point (in units)

$$4000-2000 = 2000$$

The firm will have to decide whether the Margin of Safety is adequate to satisfy its objectives.

BUDGETING

Budgeting is a planning process which involves the setting of financial targets for a given period of time to assist with the allocation of resources. Budgets may be established for various aspects of the firm's operations once they are quantifiable.

Budgets may be set for capital expenditure; sales; labour costs; and income, expenditure and profit (Master budget).

Budgets are usually based on past performance, the objectives of the firm, and the current micro- and macro-economic situation.

There are two approaches to setting a budget. These are incremental budgeting and zero based budgeting.

With incremental budgeting the firm uses the budget of the previous year as a starting point and then makes necessary adjustments downwards or upwards. For example the firm may decide to aim for higher sales and project a reduction in cost if the objective is to increase profits.

Zero-based budgeting starts with the notion that all budget items have to be justified. Each item is carefully examined to decide if it is necessary i.e. if it fits into the plan for the period under consideration.

Once the budget has been set controls are put in place during the period to ensure that the plan agreed is followed and undesirable variances are avoided. In summary Variance Analysis is conducted during the period and at the end of the period. The analysis unearths variances which are differences between budgeted and actual figures. This is a vital part of the budgeting process for the following reasons:

•   It aids analysis of the causes of deviations from the budget
•   It assists in determining changes for future budgets

A variance is positive or favourable when the actual costs are lower than expected or revenues higher than expected. On the other hand, a variance is negative or adverse when costs are higher than expected or revenues lower than expected.

RESEARCH TASKS

1. Search online for an example of the Profit and Loss Statement and Balance Sheet of a Public Limited company.
2. Contact a firm to see an example of a Bank Reconciliation.
3. Contact a company to obtain an example of a Budget
4. Calculate the acid test ratio for a company for which you have obtained the relevant financial documents.

QUESTIONS

1. Explain what is the Net Profit Margin of a firm
2. Describe the Return on Capital Employed
3. Calculate the Break Even point in units for a firm with overheads of $ 60,000 which sells a product for $ 10.00 This product incurs a variable cost of $ 5.00.
4. Explain the importance of Variance Analysis.

CHAPTER 13

MARKET STRUCTURES AND PRICE DETERMINATION

In this Chapter there will be consideration of:

(a) Perfect Competition.
(b) Monopoly and Monopolistic Competition.
(c) Oligopoly.

Also to be examined will be:

(d) Demand and Supply.
(e) The Equilibrium Price.

PERFECT COMPETITION

The following are the characteristics of Perfect Competition:

1. No single buyer can fix the final or current price.
2. No single seller, where other sellers exist, can set the market price.
3. There are numerous buyers and sellers.
4. Sellers have an intimate knowledge of conditions in the market.
5. Like sellers, buyers are extremely familiar with market conditions.
6. Products which are made available have roughly the same characteristics and will in many respects be 'standard' and similar.
7. Over time businesses can enter the market as they please.
8. Business entities and firms are free to leave the market at their choice.

In reviewing the requirements of Perfect Competition it must be borne in mind that Caribbean countries have open economies in which imports not only exceed exports but imports are produced abroad and a few distributors, usually wholesalers, bring goods to the local markets.

Some wholesalers do have exclusive rights to the importation of specific products from particular foreign sellers.

In addition some wholesalers are allowed through special permission to blend, assemble and put together inputs and components on behalf of foreign suppliers.

In light of the foregoing, when local wholesalers 'manufacture' on behalf of foreign principals and when the producers themselves are not based in the local countries the question arises as to whether the traditional chain of distribution is as strong as in the past. Highly relevant too is if this chain of distribution means much, in instances where:

i. Manufacturers and producers deal directly with local retailers.

ii.   Manufacturers and producers sell directly to consumers.

iii.   When the chain of distribution allows for more than one wholesaler and or more than one retailer to market products.

In light of the above, the question is 'Does perfect competition really exists in the real world?"

Another question is 'In light of relatively few distributors in Caribbean countries can it be said that perfect competition does exist in open Caribbean economies?

As far as market structures are concerned the concept of monopoly must be examined.

MONOPOLY

A monopoly exists when one firm dominates a particular industry.

For example in Barbados, the Barbados Light and Power Co. Ltd. is the sole provider of electricity services. The same is true with the supply of water. The Barbados Water Authority is the sole distribution of potable water. These are extreme cases but as long as a firm has excessive dominance in the market it is considered a monopoly.

MONOPOLISTIC COMPETITION

As far as monopolistic competition is concerned, there is more than one seller but sellers' products carry very special features. On account of these features competitors' products tend to be at a disadvantage in terms of:-

    (a) Quality;
    (b) Amounts made available to the market; and
    (c) Prices.

Among the attributes of monopolistic competition are:-

    1. Unrestricted access into the market in the long term.
    2. Competition among many sellers.
    3. A viable and definite differentiation among products.

Under the systems of monopolistic competition since commodities differ among competitors, increases in price levels may not cause demand to decrease. Yet a decline in price will usually cause demand to increase.

Since monopolistic competition does allow new firms to enter the market, original monopolies have to face the challenges which come about as a result of competition.

As new firms enter the market and bring competition with them, consumers do have choices among products which reveal differences in quality, price and character.

OLIGOPOLY

A dictionary definition of Oligopoly is:

> "A market situation in which control over the supply of a commodity is held by a small number of producers."

In a situation where a few firms produce basically the same product or service there is said to be perfect oligopoly.

Where the few firms in existence produce different products and can still control quantities supplied and prices, imperfect oligopoly is said to be in existence.

There also exists the concept of duopoly which means that only two firms rather than one firm or more than two firms take control of the market.

Where oligopoly exists, firms set prices but may make differential products available.

A Cartel is a kind of oligopoly in which competitors combine to work together in the interest of enhanced profits. These firms which function in cartels feel that it is in their best interest to cooperate with each other to deal with uncertain market conditions and to position themselves to attain results which would benefit participants in the Cartel.

DEMAND AND SUPPLY

THE PRICE MECHANISM
The price mechanism is the result of the actions of demand and supply interacting in the market to determine price.

The price mechanism consists of

1. Demand
2. Supply
3. Price

LAW OF DEMAND AND SUPPLY

Demand relates to the capacity and willingness of consumers to buy a product at a specific price within a given timeframe.

As regards the law of demand when price is high the quantity demanded will be low but when the reverse occurs and price is low consumers will demand more quantities.

Supply relates to the capacity and willingness of sellers to provide products (including services) at a particular price within a given timeframe.
The lower the price consumers are prepared to offer, the smaller would be the amount supplied.

However as consumers offer higher prices suppliers would be willing to supply more or greater quantities.

DEMAND

Now consider the following:

DEMAND SCHEDULE

PRICE OF PRODUCT (Per Unit)	QUANTITY DEMANDED
40	8
30	10
20	12
10	16

The above information can be plotted on what is known as a demand curve.

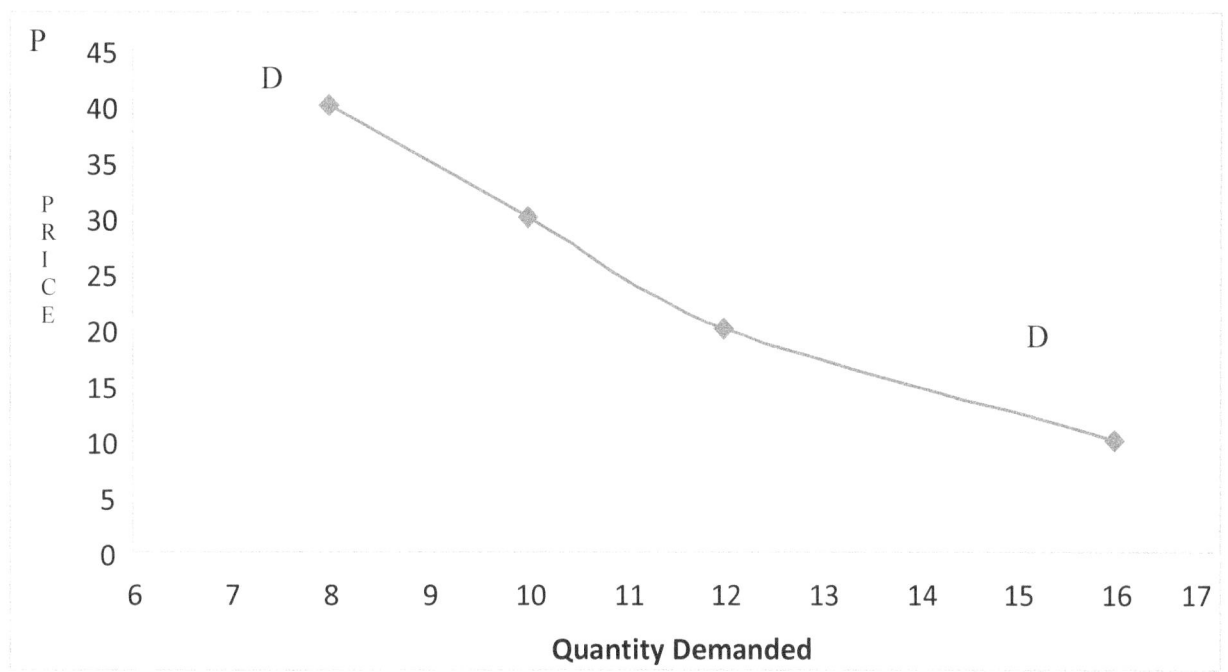

At a price of 40.00 only eight units of product are in demand whilst at a price of 10, consumers are interested in 16 units. At a price of 20 consumers are prepared to buy 12 units.

SUPPLY

PRICE OF PRODUCT (Per Unit)	QUANTITY SUPPLIED
15	9
20	12
30	15
40	20

This information can be presented in a supply curve showing the relationship between price and quantity supplied.

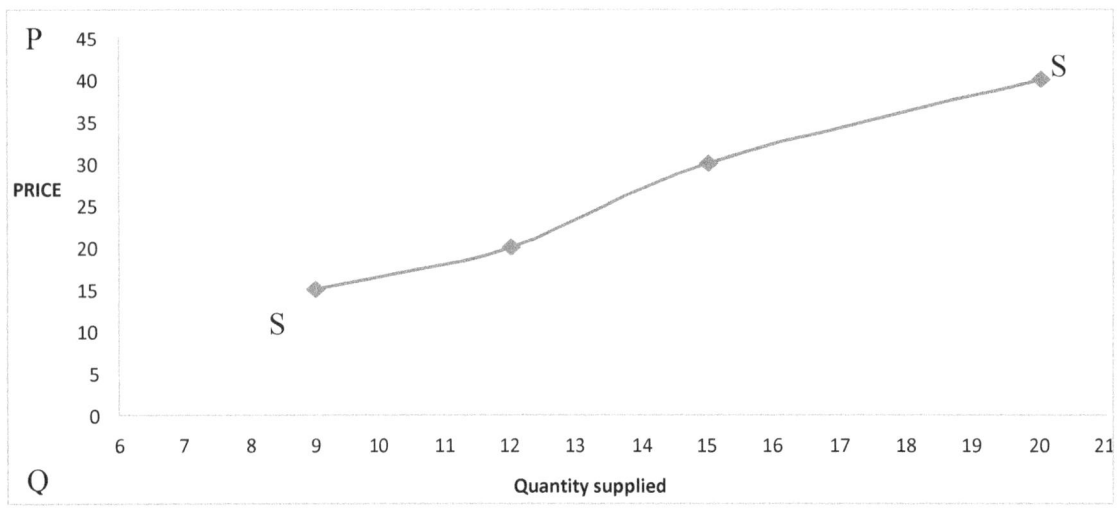

When the price is high 40 suppliers are keen to provide 20 units but when the price falls to 15 only 9 units of product are being made available by suppliers.

Now consider the below:

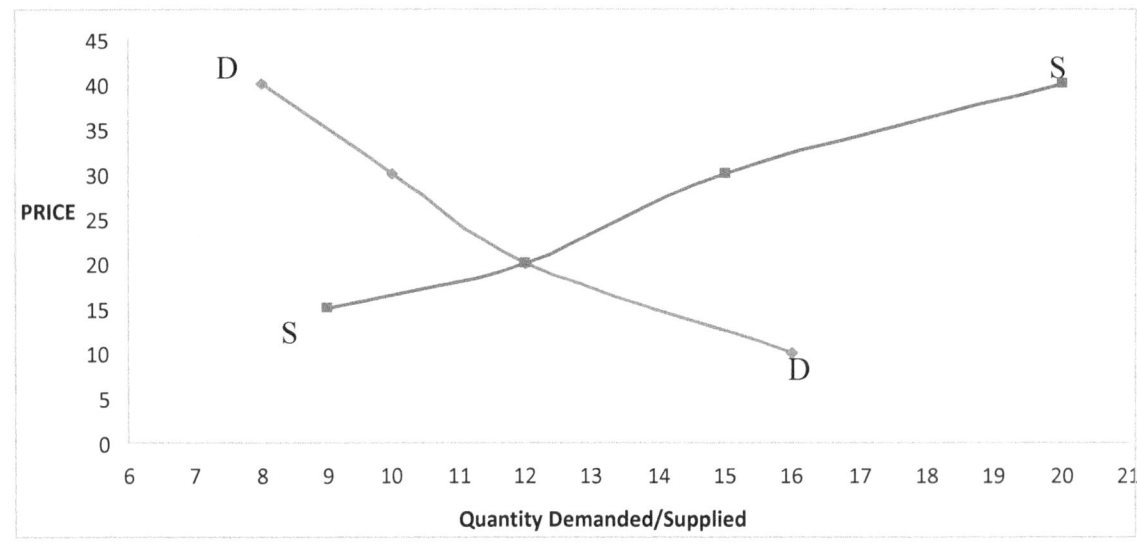

The coming together and meeting of the demand and supply curves show that at a price of 20 suppliers are making 12 units available and the demand shown by consumers is in agreement with this price and quantity.

The above paints the typical picture of the theory of demand and supply but in practice there are a number of other factors which influence demand and supply and price as well.

Reminder: Do get to appreciate what the equilibrium price is.

THE MARKET

EQUILIBRIUM PRICE

In a free competitive market there exists a price known as the equilibrium price. The equilibrium price is the price at which both buyer and supplier are agreed is their trading price. Though suppliers are willing to supply more goods at higher prices, consumers are not interested in these higher prices.

Of note though consumers are willing to buy more at cheaper prices, suppliers are not willing to sell at those cheaper prices.

Buyers are keen to buy more below the market equilibrium price and suppliers are willing to offer more above the market equilibrium price but both sides are agreed to buy and sell 12 units at a price of 20 cents.

FACTORS WHICH AFFECT DEMAND

1. Changes in the prices of complementary goods. Where the price of a complementary good goes up it can cause the demand for the 'companion good' to decrease. Where the price of complementary goods falls there can be an increase in the companion good.
2. Changes in the price(s) of substitute goods. Substitutes are competitors in the market against a wide range of goods and price changes of substitutes can affect demand.
3. Changes in styles, taste(s) and fashions if negative will cause demand to decrease. However where the changes are positive demand could increase.
4. Where consumers fear that prices will increase in the near future.
5. Where there are fears that taxes will increase.

RESEARCH TASKS

1.   Find out what is monopsony.
2.   Carefully research cartels and show how they can engage in unfair trade practices.
3.   Carefully research the concepts of elasticity of demand and elasticity
        of supply.
4.   What are substitute goods? Search for examples.
5.   What are complementary goods?

QUESTIONS

1.   Outline five features of Perfect Competition.
2.   Explain monopoly
3.   Provide two examples of monopoly.
4.   Why do some Caribbean Governments operate some
        enterprises as monopolies.
5.   Define Oligopoly.

CHAPTER 14

EVERYDAY FACTORS WHICH INFLUENCE CONSUMER BEHAVIOUR

A number of factors affect the manner in which consumers respond to given goods and services.

Among these factors are price, the cost of substitutes, quality, taste, tradition, levels of income, spending patterns and brand loyalty.

PRICE

Price can be defined as what it costs consumers to take control of goods and services. In the market place price has an exchange value and in today's world, price tends to be expressed as a monetary measure of value while money is used as a means or medium of exchange. The final seller of goods or his or her agent charges the consumer either in terms of their products' value in the market place and or what they expect, having considered both the total costs of production as well as the unit price which they wish to obtain for what they are selling. Those responsible for selling must bear their costs of production in mind, while taking into account the fact that many consumers are price sensitive. In most cases the final price per unit of production will reflect items such as the unit costs of raw materials, utilities, transport and labour among other things.

In some cases when budgeting ahead of final purchase, the consumer has to consider the price of complementary goods which are goods which go together with and are sold with one another.

For example ackee and saltfish are complementary goods. Other examples are rum and coke, engine oil and fuel for motor vehicles and such like.

THE PRICE OF SUBSTITUTES

A substitute is a commodity or service which is an alternative to another product or service.

Pork can be a substitute for beef in the open market except for those who on account of their religion or some similar reason refuse to eat pork.

Chicken can be a substitute for pork and beef.

Fish can be a substitute for the three products listed above.

If a consumer elects to purchase chicken rather than fish it may be the case either that the personal taste(s) of the consumer influence(s) the consumer's decision but more often than not, when a consumer chooses a substitute it is that the substitute is being offered at a lower price. The substitute may be of equal quality. It must be acknowledged that dependent on their incomes, many consumers are price sensitive meaning that they are not willing to spend on expensive items if cheaper ones can do.

On the other hand, consumers who are not price sensitive do not quibble over how expensive goods and services are but purchase what they want even when aware that they are paying more for goods which the price-sensitive consumer will avoid.

Persons whose incomes are high or relatively high tend to demonstrate buying behaviour which is different from that of consumers whose income is low or relatively low.

Of note some miserly consumers who have high incomes are as price sensitive as the poorer elements in their communities, no doubt because they wish to increase their savings.

QUALITY

If quality is about the degree or standard of excellence of a commodity or service or carries particular defining and distinguishing attributes, the conclusion can be reached that goods and services which are very good and excellent will be in great demand.

Many producers aim to satisfy the market with products that:

 (a) Are attractive.
 (b) Serve useful purposes.
 (c) Last for lengthy periods of time.
 (d) In the case of machinery last long while being economical to service.
 (e) Attract after-sales service.
 (f) Are durable.

Some consumers do not mind paying extra for goods of excellent quality.

TASTE

This is definitely one of the principal factors influencing consumer behaviour. Taste means a liking or preference for something.

Different people have different tastes and very personal subjective 'reasons' determine taste.

When a consumer is able to derive considerable satisfaction (utility) from consuming goods and services this consumer will always be willing to buy these things to which she or he is attracted.

Quite often style and fashion, especially when they exhibit beauty and excellent quality are the reasons why consumers select certain goods.

Certain occasions e.g. a wedding require the use of appropriate style and fashion.

There are instances when consumers imitate friends by consuming the identical products which their peers are making use of. 'Keeping up with the Joneses' does influence consumer behaviour.

TRADITION.

In many respects 'tradition' refers to customs many of which have been practiced for years. For example at carnival in Trinidad and Tobago and elsewhere, special costumes are worn but when carnival is over the costumes are discarded.

Practitioners of the Christian religion especially Catholics prefer to consume fish on Good Friday and so the demand for red meats and even chicken decreases on Good Friday. Indeed some Caribbean nationals only use fish on Fridays outside of Good Friday.

The consumption of ham and turkey at Christmas is another example of how customs and tradition matter in consumer behaviour.

Particular religions dissuade their followers from consuming particular commodities, e.g. Muslins and Seventh-Day Adventists do not eat port nor pork products.

LEVELS OF WAGES AND SALARIES

Income is an important determinant of spending.

As a general rule the higher the income the more products and services will be purchased. Those whose take home pay is (very) high will not only buy food and other essentials but will have enough financial resources to acquire luxuries.

Where in a given economy income is low then people can usually afford little more than food and basic goods, e.g. medicine for survival.

As consumers' incomes increase they will tend to spend more and may be able to buy a wide range of products.

When real incomes decrease, whether through inflation or other causes consumers are limited or restricted in the choices they are now forced to exercise.

Instances exist when as consumers' incomes increase to higher levels they make adjustments in their spending by purchasing less or fewer goods of a particular kind. Inferior goods e.g. salt, are commodities of a nature that as people grow richer their demand for such, falls.

Giffen goods on the other hand are commodities, which as they increase in price witness an increase in demand.

SPENDING PATTERNS

Different consumers have different levels of income, different tastes and their own preferences.

Spending patterns are often determined not only by the ordinary or normal market conditions but by instances where consumers, based especially on their levels of income have to prioritize their spending. Low income consumers spend a greater proportion of their income on food and basics while those persons whose incomes are high tend to spend significant sums on luxurious and expensive items. On occasions where there are SALES and DISCOUNTS consumers respond by purchasing 'bargains'.

The parent(s) of a baby will spend more on baby products like milk formulae, baby foods and pampers. This will cause the demand for baby products among mothers and parents to increase.

At the other end of the scale is the position of the elderly. Many senior citizens find that a sizeable amount of their incomes is spent on medicines and medical supplies. This creates a specific pattern of spending in this particular market segment or target group.

Of note many retired people go traveling on cruises. This is so because some senior citizens can afford boat and shipping cruises because they have completed their mortgage payments and hire-purchase bills and so have enough income and purchasing power to afford to go on cruises.

BRAND LOYALTY

A brand is its own peculiar description of a product. Effective branding attracts the attention of consumers to products. When the brand and its accompanying label prove enticing the other considerations which will matter will be product presentation, price and quality. Often a brand has been in existence for years, e.g. Ovaltine, Milo and Red Rose tea.

Many consumers select only certain brands and ignore the fact that there are other products of almost identical quality and utility available in the market.

PATENTS

Relevant to the matter of branding is the presence of some patents which are tacked on to the brand. The question of the nature and purpose of patents is one worthy of examination.

A patent is the exclusive proprietary right to an invention and in many respects a patent is an asset and is property.

A patent confers:

(a) Exclusive rights to exploit an invention.
(b) The right to register and license an invention.
(c) A legal right to so assert a monopoly on an invention as to take legal action against anyone who infringes the patent.
(d) A deterrence which persuades unauthorized persons from using the patent.

Patents may be applied to:
(a) New products.
(b) Changes and improvements to existing products.
(c) Unique processes in manufacture and production.
(d) New scientific materials; and
(e) Electronic components.

ANGOSTURA BITTERS produced in Trinidad and Tobago is an example of a unique Caribbean product which has been patented.

Discussing patents raises the issue of trademarks.

TRADEMARKS

Many brands are characterized by trademarks. Trademarks are descriptions or products using names, messages and emblems to describe products.

Like patents, trademarks are most effective when registered with the government department which regulates intellectual property.

One purpose of registered trademarks is to give a special identity to products. Another purpose is to prevent competitors from 'passing off' their products as their own and to prevent unfair competitive behaviour.

If Angus Ltd. has the registered right to use the term 'Magic' as its trademark then other producers cannot use the term 'Magic'. This is especially so in instances where competing products are similar to what Angus Ltd. is producing. If Angus Ltd. produces 'Magic' soap then others cannot brand or label their soaps 'Magic'.

However if Dennis Ltd. is producing motor vehicles – a far cry from soaps – then 'Magic' may be permitted to describe the vehicles because Dennis Ltd. is not passing off its products in competition nor in conflict with what Angus Ltd. is producing.

Trademarks do not only identify products but where a trademark has come to be associated with products known for quality, reliability, good prices, after sales service and the like, trademarks can generate goodwill and increases in sales for the holder of the trademarks.

Trademarks are property and can therefore be assigned.

The holder of a trademark can contract with an assignee to allow the assignee a franchise.

A franchise is special permission granted by the holder of the trademark to a licensee to allow the latter to label their product(s) with the trademark of the true original holder of the trademark.

RESEARCH TASKS

1. Examine factors which affect disposable income.
2. Identify examples of (a) Patents (b) trademarks.
3. Identify examples of complementary goods not mentioned in this chapter.
4. Provide examples of Giffen goods

QUESTIONS

1.   "Some consumers are more worried by high prices than others…."

   (a)   What type of consumer would be concerned by high prices?
   (b)   Apart from price, consider three other attributes of goods and services which would appeal to consumers.
   (c)   Why do some consumers NOT bother about prices?

2.   Distinguish a patent from a trademark.
3.   What is a franchise?
4.   Why as some people's incomes increase they tend to buy less of some commodities. Provide examples to illustrate your answer.

CHAPTER 15

CONSUMER PROTECTION

WHO IS A CONSUMER?

In Trinidad and Tobago a 'consumer' …is a person to whom goods or services are sought to be supplied in the course of a business which is carried on by the person supplying or seeking to supply them and does not receive or seek to receive the goods or services in the course of business carried on by her or him. (the consumer)

What this means is that where a person is a user of goods and services **OUTSIDE** of any business carried on by the purchaser then that person is a consumer.

This suggests that a consumer is one who buys for personal use.

Antigua and Barbuda in defining 'consumer' does not really have identical wording of the term but there is **NOT** much marked difference between how these two countries see 'consumer'.

Jamaica's legislation does add to the measures outlined by Antigua and Barbuda and Trinidad and Tobago by indicating that a commercial undertaking which buys consumer goods is also a consumer. The average person will recognize who a consumer is even when unaware of the legal definitions of the term 'consumer'.

REASONS WHY CONSUMERS NEED PROTECTION

(a) Products and Services may be the wrong items which the consumer had paid for.

(b) Goods and Services may have been entirely different from how they were advertised.

(c) Some suppliers and providers of goods and services often refuse to exchange items returned to them by consumers.

(d) Some suppliers and providers refuse to refund consumers.

(e) Consumers are often the victims of misleading advertisements.

(f) Some goods are defective and unsafe.

(g) Some businesses offer poor or no after sales service.

(h) Some suppliers and producers do not deliver on time.

(i) Some businesses refuse to hear the complaints of consumers.

(j) Many consumers cannot afford the legal costs of bringing action against delinquent suppliers and providers.

SOME GENERAL RIGHTS OF CONSUMERS

1. The right to accurate information on products and services.
2. The right to ask questions about products and services.
3. The right to choose.
4. The right to complain on the spot or within a reasonable time when consumers have concerns.
5. The right to safe products and services.
6. The right under Health Services rules to clean surroundings when shopping.
7. The right to turn to the appropriate Government Department or Public Officer for assistance with their concerns.
8. Where the consumer is not at fault the right to legal support and protection.
9. Guarantees that products and services are of the right quality and size and that the products and services meet descriptions as have been advertised.

In practice the above rights have been bolstered and reinforced by specific pieces of legislation passed in Caribbean territories in the last fifteen years or so.

MODERN METHODS OF CONSUMER PROTECTION BY GOVERNMENTS

Governments have undertaken several steps to afford protection to consumers.

Among these are created positions like the Director of Consumer Guidance (in Trinidad and Tobago), the Director of Consumer Affairs (Antigua and Barbuda), the establishment of a Consumer Protection Commission in the Bahamas and The Fair Trading Commission of Barbados along with other Agencies. Other jurisdictions have equivalent institutions and agencies to protect consumers.

Generally these functionaries are to ensure that there are no unfair business practices that infringe on consumer rights, that there is product safety and that there are no unfair contract terms that can cause damage, expense and loss to consumers.

In Barbados there is the Office of Public Counsel which has responsibility for applying relevant consumer legislation.

The Consumer Guarantees Act of Barbados sets out minimum standards for all goods and services which are sold for personal and domestic use.

In addition in Barbados, retailers bear responsibility for the guarantee of the quality of goods they sell.

Similar rules exist across the region.

MODERN CARIBBEAN METHODS OF CONSUMER PROTECTION BY GOVERNMENTS

It is now the law in most territories that suppliers and providers cannot post "No refunds" notices and are duty bound to exchange returned goods.

Under Health Services rules, persons who sell food must have genuine health certificates and inspectors go around to ensure that the laws are upheld.

In addition in some territories there are Price Controls on basic items like baby foods, milk, flour and other basic food items.

Weights and Measures legislation requiring fair and accurate measures have been in existence for many years. These are revised and updated from time to time.

Governments have over time to time insisted on quality and value for money.

Most Caricom countries have Standards Institutions which assess standards, quality and specifications and which work with other agencies to ensure fairness in the market place.

HOW CONSUMERS CAN PROTECT THEMSELVES

Consumers ought to:-
- Gather information on products and services.
- Spend time exploring and monitoring what is being offered for Sale.
- Avoid impulse buying.
- Ascertain if so-called sales and discounts are genuine.
- Deal with suppliers who are known to be honest and fair.
- Check labels carefully to gain proper information.
- Compare substitutes and competing products and services.
- Where circumstances require, ensure that after sales service(s) are offered by suppliers.
- Where possible, join and work with non-government consumer bodies and agencies.
- Educate themselves widely on market conditions.

HOW SHOULD CONSUMERS COMPLAIN

1. Inform the supplier, provider or retailer about the problem giving details.
2. If there is a complaints wicket or department go there and lodge the complaint.
3. If no redress is offered at first attempt, find ways of asking for the manner in which the seller deals with complaints.
4. Write a letter to the Chief Executive Officer or Manager with the details of the

consumer's complaints.

5. If no redress or satisfaction has been granted by the seller or store notify the Director of Fair Trading or the Ministry of Consumer Affairs. Where necessary ask the appropriate government department for a full investigation.

6. When there is legal aid available or someone like a Public Counsel, make use of their services.

The consumer ought never to be afraid to seek help. In this modern era most businesses – operating in a competitive commercial environment – will probably try to assist.

The consumer should keep notes and details of the complaint to go further if doing so is necessary.

Seek the assistance of Non-Governmental Consumer Organizations.

When the consumer has a just, genuine complaint they should not hesitate in making it.

STANDARDS INSTITUTIONS

Since the 1970's Caribbean Governments have been gradually establishing Standards Institutions similar to the Barbados National Standards Institution (BNSI).

The primary objectives of Standards Institutions are:-
- To assist Caribbean industries to produce goods and services of proper marketable quality.
- To encourage manufacturers to practice quality control systems at every level of the production process.
- To position consumers to be sure that products and services in the market place are of acceptable quality and that such quality can be independently verified.
- To empower manufacturers to improve the quality, reliability and soundness of products.
- To seek to inspire Caricom countries to have certain basic mandatory standards of quality.

The Barbados National Standards Institution has introduced certification marks vouching for the compliance of businesses with the standards laid down by the BNSI.

The work of Standards Institutions in the Caribbean has sought to do the following:
(a)   Bring about full metrification;
(b)   Require producers to offer quality;
(c)   Keep abreast of international rules governing trade; and
(d)   Use international technical assistance.

THE CARICOM REGIONAL ORGANISATION FOR STANDARDS AND QUALITY (CROSQ)

Established by Caricom, the Caribbean Regional Organisation for Standards and Quality (CROSQ) has as its mission statement:

"The promotion and development of standards and standards related activities to facilitate international competitiveness and the sustainable production of goods and services within the CARICOM Single Market and Economy (CSME) for the enhancement of social and economic development."

Member States of CROSQ are:-
Antigua and Barbuda
The Bahamas
Barbados
Belize
Dominica
Grenada
Guyana
Jamaica
Montserrat
St. Kitts and Nevis
St. Lucia
St. Vincent and the Grenadines
Suriname
Trinidad and Tobago

The broad aims and objectives of CROSQ are:

- To promote the development of standards and the recognition of technical regulations.
- To encourage the recognition of internally accredited certification systems.
- To facilitate the achievement of international competitiveness of regional goods and services by fostering a culture of quality in regional enterprises.
- To contribute, through its operations, to the preservation of the environment and conservation of the national resources of the CARICOM Single Market and Economy (CSME).
- To provide guidance to organizations and bodies of the CSME including, but not limited to disputes settlement.
- To provide and protect the interests of States, Parties and Associate Members in regional and international standards fora.
- To promote the awareness of standards-related matters including technical regulations, conformity assessment procedures and metrology.

CROSQ through its Council must report to Caricom's Council for Trade and Economic Development (COTED) once a year.

Much as CROSQ's mandate appears to stress quality standards for businesses in the region CROSQ's link within the world beyond Caricom can cause inflows of information for consumer education generally.

Under trade liberalization, CROSQ can act not only to protect regional businesses but also those who buy from these businesses.

RESEARCH TASKS

1. Find out why non-governmental Consumer Bodies have not done well in the Caribbean.
2. Research the major consumer legislation in your territory.
3. How effective is such legislation.
4. Propose three measures to improve the protection of Caribbean consumers.

QUESTIONS

1. Provide a clear description of the term 'consumer'.
2. Why is consumer education important?
3. Outline three steps a consumer can take to protect their interests.
4. Indicate four policies which Caribbean governments have introduced to protect consumers
5. Suggest two other measures which would be of benefit to Caribbean Consumers.
6. Explain 'caveat emptor'.
7. How relevant is the concept of 'caveat emptor' these days?

CHAPTER 16

MONEY, BANKING AND FINANCE

This Chapter deals with Institutions which play a part in the financial sector of Caribbean economies and commences with discussion on Central Banks.

CENTRAL BANKS
FUNCTIONS

1. They are responsible for the issue of all currency and coins issued in their countries.
2. They are Bankers to their Governments.
3. They are Bankers to Commercial (Retail) Banks.
4. They are responsible for Government's monetary policy.
5. Some of them run Export Credit Guarantee Schemes to facilitate exports.
6. They are lenders of last resort.
7. They collect and manage their countries foreign reserves.
8. They provide limited banking services to special categories of persons.
9. They monitor the operations of Commercial Banks to prevent them from breaching Central Bank rules.
10. They are important advisers to Government on particular economic matters.

HOW CENTRAL BANKS CAN INFLUENCE POLICY

By making adjustments to the money supply e.g. they can require commercial banks to increase their deposits with Central Banks thereby reducing the total amount of money in circulation in the economy. When the total amount of money in the economy is reduced, aggregate national demand for goods and services will decrease. Where the demand for foreign imports decreases, less foreign exchange will leave the economy resulting in savings of foreign exchange with positive implications for the reduction of fiscal deficit(s) etc. and balance of payment problems.

Where as a result of a decrease in the money supply, fewer national goods and services are bought, the results may be two-fold, going in opposite directions:

As a result of a decrease in the money supply there would be an ease in the pressure on the foreign reserves because fewer imports would be brought into the country.

There are occasions when a reduction in money supply can affect local production and sales by decreasing the demand for goods. A decrease in the demand for local goods can actually cause local businesses to lose income which may lead to layoffs, reduction in staff and a decrease in local output.

The above shows defensive measures Central Banks could use to decrease national demand to ease pressure off a country's foreign reserves.

COMMERCIAL BANKING

General

Commercial banks play a most important part in business, commerce and trade. Like insurance, advertising, transport, wholesaling and retailing, banking can be considered to be a very special facilitator of business.

The existence of banks does allow firms and individuals to benefit from banking services which can assist in ensuring better and more efficient performance by these firms and individuals.

Some services offered by commercial banks:

- Deposits
- Safety Deposits
- Loans
- Overdrafts
- The sale of foreign exchange
- Credit transfers
- Current accounts
- Standing orders
- Bank drafts
- Financial advice
- Credit cards
- Debit cards

Deposits

Commercial banks accept deposits from the public. These deposits are held to the credit of individual clients but the hard fact of the situation is that the hundreds of deposits made in the commercial banking sector do permit such a build-up of cash and funds, that the banks could lend out some of these resources which represent the savings or at least some of the savings of clients. Interest on deposits is generally low, but there exists a special type of deposit known as a fixed deposit by which the client agrees to allow his or her money to be on the bank as a fixed amount with the proviso that if the client should try to take funds from a fixed deposit prematurely, he/she would be penalized by having to spend some of the money deposited as special bank charges. Fixed Deposits carry higher interest than ordinary savings accounts.

In discussing deposits it is necessary to mention that almost all banks have safety deposit boxes where traders in particular, can deposit and store money in a bank often overnight, rather than leaving it on the premises of his or her businesses.

Loans

Banks lend money and in so doing charge interest. If banks lend money wantonly without protecting their interest, they would lose substantial sums when borrowers default.

In practice banks take certain things into account and insist on collateral security.

FACTORS TAKEN INTO ACCOUNT WHEN LENDING MONEY

      (a)   Length of time the applicant has been working.
      (b)   Property owned by applicant.
      (c)   The applicant's cash savings.
      (d)   The applicant's borrowing history.
      (e)   The applicant's reputation and standing in the community.

FORMS OF SECURITY

      (a) Shares in companies
      (b) Cash surrender value of insurance policies.
      (c) Freehold title to land.
      (d) Very lengthy leasehold.
      (e) Solid wall structures of value owned by the applicant(s).
      (f) Expensive valuables and assets.

CURRENT ACCOUNT SERVICES

Current Accounts and personal chequeing accounts allow payments to be made instead of cash. Most firms and individuals recognize that there are great risks having large amounts of cash on their premises. Instead they deposit their cash with banks and can write cheques up to the amounts, (taking into account bank and administrative charges), which have been left with the banks. If Govindra puts $15,000 in the bank at first it appears that he can write cheques up to $15,000 but he has to make allowance for the stamp duty and bank charges which will be extracted by the bank in servicing his chequeing or current account.

OVERDRAFTS

Overdrafts are connected to current accounts.

Consider this scenario: Alfred has a chequeing account that has a zero balance but writes a cheque for $5,000 which his bank the PSTR Bank Ltd. pays to the payee to whom Alfred has written the cheque. Alfred has literally overdrawn his current account by $5,000 and would have had to have been permitted by the bank to overdraw his current account by at least $5,000. Alfred would have had to request an overdraft to facilitate this transaction.

An overdraft is formalized when a commercial bank permits a client to take more from his current or chequeing account than he/she has on such an account. The effect of an overdraft is that the bank has loaned funds via a chequeing account up to a certain limit. The interest rates on overdrafts tend to be higher than on ordinary loans and before any commercial bank grants an overdraft to a client, the client must have proper collateral security or business assets or a strong reputation in their community. Where a client writes a cheque but has no funds at the Bank and has no overdraft facilities the cheque is said to be a dishonored cheque because the bank would not honour it.

BANK DRAFTS

There are occasions when a client has to make a payment, often by post. Sending actual cash through the mail is risky. Banks are prepared to issue bank drafts on behalf of clients where clients are posting payments or ordering goods and services by mail. A bank draft is a document which guarantees that the bank which has issued it will make a payment on behalf of the client who has requested the draft from the bank. Bank drafts tend to be safer than cheques.

MORE ABOUT CURRENT ACCOUNTS AND CHEQUES

Over the years banks have applied various features to cheques and in today's world there are:

- Bearer cheques
- Open cheques
- Crossed cheques.
- 'Payee only' cheques.

BEARER CHEQUES

Bearer cheques which are rather old-fashioned and hardly in use, do not name the payee directly. They are written 'Pay bearer' so if they are lost anyone can cash them. They are risky which explains why they are hardly used nowadays.

OPEN CHEQUES

Open cheques bear no crossing and are therefore not restricted to any special terms or to an account. They are usually encashable over the counter so long as it can be proved that the person who wrote the cheque (the drawer) has enough funds in his/ her account.

ENDORSING A CHEQUE

When a person is paid a cheque that person must sign the cheque on its back. Such signing is called endorsing the cheque.

If the person takes a cheque to a bank other than one where the chequeing account is located, that person would normally be required to deposit it until it is cleared. If this person has money on his/her bank but this bank does not hold and operate the chequeing account for the person paying the cheque, the payee will be paid cash that is, the cheque will be cashed and then if it proves worthless the bank will deduct funds and expense from the account of the payee.

CROSSED CHEQUES

A crossed cheque is one which is marked to indicate that it should be deposited into a payee's bank account. It is not immediately cashed by a bank over the counter.

'PAYEE ONLY' CHEQUES

These are cheques which are stamped 'payee only' to indicate that the cheque cannot be accessed by any person other than the payee. It must be deposited in the payee's bank account.

STANDING ORDER

A Standing Order comes into being when the client of the bank gives the bank instructions to make a payment on a given date for a fixed sum of money. For example, Juliette owes the FGH Bank Ltd. $4,000.00 and has given this bank authority to deduct the fixed sum of $200 on every 28th day of every month until the loan is paid off.

CREDIT TRANSFERS

A Credit Transfer must never be confused with a Standing Order. A credit transfer is effected when there is a transfer of a sum of money from one account to another account and can be done at any time, while the standing order is always payable on a specific date.

CREDIT CARDS

A credit card is a payment card issued to users as a system of payment using a line of credit granted by the issuer of the card. Usually the line of credit is provided with the expectation that the holder of the card will repay money used plus an interest fee for use of the service in a timely fashion. Late payment of funds attracts high interest charges. The convenience of using a credit card for most business transactions makes it a popular choice of consumers who avoid travelling with large sums of cash.

DEBIT CARDS

A debit card is a bank card which enables the holder of the card to access funds in his/her bank account to electronically deposit in a supplier's account to pay for items purchased. It avoids having to travel with cash or cheque book.

CREDIT UNIONS

Credit Unions are financial cooperatives. Originally credit unions would take in money from members referring to such money as 'shares'. Out of these 'shares' when fully totaled up, some money would be lent to individual members.

Today credit unions accept savings (shares) from members and some large credit unions also accept deposits.

Some credit unions have enough financial assets to advance large loans and mortgages.
One peculiarity of credit unions is that they constantly raise capital usually on a monthly or other periodic basis.

Caribbean governments have been allowing income tax concessions to persons who save in credit unions. Credit Unions apply the principles of:
(a)   Open membership.
(b)   Democratic Control.
(c)   Fraternity.

It is a fact that many large credit unions compete with banks and insurance companies for savings from the public but commercial banks tend to offer a wider range of services than credit unions.

THE CARIBBEAN DEVELOPMENT BANK (CDB)

By an agreement signed on October 18th, 1969 the Caribbean Development Bank came into being on January 26th, 1970.

The functions of the CDB are:-

1.   To assist its borrowing member countries (BMCS) to optimize the use of their resources, develop their economies and expand production and trade.
2.   To promote private and public investment, encourage the development of the financial upturn in the region and facilitate business activity and expansion.
3.   To mobilize financial resources from within and outside of the Caricom region.
4.   To provide technical assistance (T.A.) to its regional borrowing members.
5.   To support regional and local financial institutions and a regional market for credit and savings.
6.   To support and stimulate the development of capital markets in the region.

The CDB's charter itself empowers this important Banking Institution to "contribute to the harmonious economic growth and development of the member countries in the Caribbean and to promote economic cooperation and integration among them, having special and urgent regard to the needs of the less developed member of the region.

The Bank's current mission statement reads as follows:

"CDB intends to be the leading catalyst for development resources in the Region working in an efficient, responsive and collaborative manner with our BMC's and other development partners towards the systematic reduction of poverty in their countries through social and economic development."

In practice over the years the CDB has funded projects in –

- Agriculture
- Livestock
- Fisheries
- Forestry
- Marketing
- Manufacturing
- Mining
- Refining
- Tourism
- Export Services
- Transportation
- Housing
- Education
- Power and Energy
- Water and Sewerage
- Infrastructure

Out of concern that poverty exists in Caricom, projects aimed at the reduction of poverty have also received support.

Many countries in Caricom including Barbados, Belize, Grenada, Jamaica, St. Kitts/Nevis and the Turks and Caicos along with Antigua/Barbuda have borrowed from the CDB.

The Bahamas, Montserrat and Trinidad and Tobago have received financial support from the CDB for various projects.

It must be noted that the CDB is an associate institution of Caricom. The CDB therefore upholds the standards and objectives of the Caribbean Community (and recently) of the CSME.

STOCK EXCHANGES

The Stock Exchange of Caribbean territories, Jamaica, Barbados and Trinidad and Tobago facilitate the buying and selling of shares and securities.

Any business whose stocks and shares are sold on a Stock Exchange is taken to be a public (limited) company.

Certain essential steps must be followed for the Stock Exchanges to accept or list companies.

So long as approval is granted for stocks, shares and securities to be traded then members of the public can sell and buy shares.

It is not the practice for members of the public to be allowed to come on the floor of stock exchanges and so trade in shares and stocks and securities has to be done through brokers.

Consider the below:

Joanne holds $4,000 in shares in the EFG Ltd. and wishes to sell them. Joanne must find an approved broker to sell the shares on her behalf.
Market forces influence the prices and values of stocks and shares.

It is possible one day for a share to sell at $2 and the very next day sell at $4. The laws of demand and supply definitely operate on the stock market.

Persons interested in Stock Market Activity

Certain terms are used to describe those who invest on the stock market.

For example: A "bull" buys shares now with the aim of selling them when their value and price go up.

"Bears" sell shares today expecting that market changes in the future would allow them to buy back these shares at cheaper prices.

Stags are speculators who love to risk their luck by investing in brand new shares which come onto the market.

RESEARCH TASKS

1. Find out the various charges which clients must pay for services and Commercial banks.
2. Research the concept of 'interest' closely. How would interest differ from stamp duty?
3. Research withholding taxes.
4. What are bank notes?
5. Compare and contrast the services offered by Commercial Banks with those offered by Credit Unions.
6. What is liquidity reserve ratio(s)?

QUESTIONS

1. Outline five functions of the Central bank.
2. Provide examples as to how Central Banks can influence the policies of Government.
3. Outline three functions of Credit Unions.
4. Tom wishes to have an Overdraft Facility with his bank. Lionel as Bank Manager is to interview Tom shortly. Structure an interview between Tom and Lionel.
5. Carefully define and describe 'collateral'.
6. Indicate three ways by which the Caribbean Development Bank can facilitate development in Caricom.

CHAPTER 17

INSURANCE

DISTINCTION BETWEEN ASSURANCE AND INSURANCE

In the early years, many firms which sold life insurance were known as Assurance Societies or Assurance Companies.

Assurance comes from the word 'Assure'. It could be expected that a father or mother would want on their death that their children and offspring should have enough financial protection to be assured of being established in life.

To take an example, Mr. Sumrah buys life insurance (assurance) and for forty years pays insurance premiums in installments of $45 per fortnight. Mr. Sumrah is assured by his Insurers that on his death $45,000 will be the minimum guaranteed sum of money for his wife and children.

What Mr. Sumrah has done is to buy insurance on his life during his life with the expectation that when he dies, financial benefits would go to his family.

To the extent that everybody dies assurance is insurance bought with foresight of an event which is bound to happen.

Insurance on the other hand is protection viz. financial protection against risks which could happen but which do not necessarily have to happen.

If outside of coverage on the lives of humans, insurers decided to offer coverage on things which were certain to happen the prospect is that these insurers would go broke.

In the world of Insurance, there exist Life Insurance Companies and Non-Life Insurance Companies also known as General Insurance Companies.

LIFE INSURANCE COMPANIES

These insure people and sell various policies designed to provide financial comfort and compensation in the event of injury, illness and death.

GENERAL INSURANCE COMPANIES

These insure assets, property and offer protection against particular risks, often the risks are associated with business activity.

MUTUAL INSURANCE COMPANIES

These are Insurance Companies whose capital is provided directly by funds owned by policyholders. Mutual Insurance Companies do not raise funds on the stock market or by seeking publicly to attract investment.

Some forms of Insurance are compulsory:

COMPULSORY FORMS OF INSURANCE

Social Security Insurance also called National Insurance is compulsory. This means that in countries which have social security, persons serving in the workforce have to pay part of their earnings to a central fund out of which monies called benefits and grants are paid. Among the benefits paid by social security schemes in the Caribbean are Sickness Benefits, Maternity Benefits, Funeral Grants, Disability Benefits, Invalidity Benefits and Contributory Pensions. Readers should carefully research how National Insurance and Social Security work in their home countries. Readers should seek to discover the difference between disability and invalidity benefits where with the former an employee may be expected to recover from illness so as to work again, while with the latter there can be no prospect of an insured person being able to work again.

Motor Insurance is another form of compulsory insurance. Third party insurance is mandatory requiring owners of motor vehicles to have enough insurance to protect third parties such as passengers and other motorists as well as pedestrians who may be injured in vehicular accidents. If a person's vehicle is insured third party only, only those outside of the owner himself or herself will be protected against accident. However with comprehensive coverage even the owner is covered against accidents subject to any exception in their policies.

IMPORTANT CONCEPTS AND TERMS IN LIFE INSURANCE

Proposal

This is the application by a person who is seeking insurance and its form requires important data indeed full particulars concerning age and state of health and other relevant information.

Insurable Interest

Anyone seeking insurance must show a relationship to the risk being insured. You can insure yourself.

Insurable Risk

The risk to be insured must be real and measurable. Insurance companies have a way based on factors like age, life expectancy and of putting a reasonable value in money on the various policies which they sell.

Premium

This is the money which an insured party must pay to the Insurance Company. Most premiums are payable yearly but increasingly more flexibility is allowed where premiums may be paid at other intervals. However with Social Security and National Insurance 'contributions' is used rather than premiums.

Utmost Good Faith

The person seeking insurance must tell their Insurer the whole truth about the risks being insured. The Insurance Company too must provide truthful accurate information to the Insured party.

Statistical Basis

Every very experienced executive, middle manager and underwriter and or agent of any insurer will say that all insurance companies based on actuarial advice, could make sizeable payments to settle claims and still remain profitable.

Insurance companies set premiums and create a pool of money out of which claims, entitlements and payments can be made. They do so by ensuring proper premiums are set, weeding out bad risks, earning funds through investments and putting actuarial advice into effect. Under subrogation there is cost recovery, so that even after paying a claim the Insurer can sell assets as scrap or damaged and 'earn' funds in the process.

Just Claim

When some unforeseen event occurs which is beyond the control of the Insured party and where the Insured party is not making a fraudulent claim, the insurer will pay compensation on the basis of the claim.

Benefit

This is a term used in National Insurance and Social Security and examples of benefit are sickness, maternity, survivor and certain pension benefits.

Subrogation

This applies solely to General Insurance or Non-Life Insurance – where insured property is damaged and a successful claim is made to replace it, the damaged property immediately becomes the property of the Insurer.

Indemnity

This comes from the word 'indemnify' and an indemnity is designed to put the insured person in the same financial position he or she would have been in if the insured person had not suffered loss. It is compensation paid by the Insurer.

Actuary

An actuary is a special statistician who advises insurers on every aspect of given risks including mortality, frequency of the occurrence of certain risks etc.

Contribution

Where the same asset is insured more than once and a claim is made the insured person cannot claim a windfall. So if John insures his house whose value is $150,000 with two different insurers and the house is destroyed, John is not allowed to get $300,000. Each insurer, under the principle of contribution will pay $75,000.00.

A distinction between 'contribution' as used in social security and national insurance has to be made here. With social security 'contribution' is like a premium payment.

TYPES OF POLICY AND COVERAGE AVAILABLE IN THE GENERAL INSURANCE INDUSTRY

Burglary

Coverage against the theft of valuables, money and other property.

Public Liability

Insurance Protection to compensate members of the public who suffer losses and injury while dealing with the insured.

Occupiers' Liability

Where businesses as occupiers experience accidents on their premises certain policies cover occupier's liability. If the businesses had to pay directly large amounts of money on their own, their businesses would have to pay out so much money is to suffer financial setbacks.

Fire

General Insurance Companies accept premiums in exchange for coverage of many risks, including fire. If a business experiences a fire and it is insured against this event compensation is paid to the business.

Hurricane and Flood

Businesses can purchase insurance policies that provide indemnity where damage and losses result from hurricane and floods.

Part Comprehensive

A part comprehensive insurance policy provides indemnity for a range of risks but leave out certain risks and perils. E.g. Some policies which provide protection against hurricanes leave out burglary and flood.

Full Comprehensive

A full comprehensive policy covers all the possible risks that face a business or household. The premiums for such will be high.

TYPES OF POLICY AND COVERAGE AVAILABLE IN LIFE INSURANCE

Term life is a relatively inexpensive form of insurance which provides a guaranteed death benefit but no cash value. This form of insurance normally lasts for specific time periods.

Whole Life insurance provides life-long protection and builds cash values which may be accessed if the need arises.

An Endowment policy is designed to offer a lump sum after a specific term or on death of the insured person to provide a death benefit to the beneficiary.

A Life Annuity is a policy which provides the holder with a series of payments at fixed intervals paid while the purchaser is alive.

A Pension Plan is a policy which allows the owner to earn a pension on retirement.

Group Life insurance covers a group of people who are usually employees of a firm. The firm pays the premium (or most of it) and the policy is usually a kind of term insurance for specific periods and provides death benefits.

TYPES OF RISK LIFE INSURERS AVOID

Outside of the Social Security Schemes in the Caribbean which require workers to be insured with state agencies, there are many private insurance companies which are in the market to make profit. These privately owned insurers would avoid risks which would force them to make high payments.

Here is a list of some of the risks private insurance companies would avoid or require the insured to pay substantial amounts of money as premiums:

(a) Persons who repeatedly take part in dangerous activities
(b) Persons exposed to constant threat to their health.

(c) Persons suffering from terminal diseases.

(d) Persons who are heavy smokers, drinkers and drug users.

(e) Persons who are clearly telling lies.

Some persons like aircraft pilots, soldiers, racing drivers, policemen and firemen could still qualify for insurance subject to special conditions and rates.

HOW INSURANCE RELATES OF BUSINESS ACTIVITY

Imagine a business which is worth $30,000,000 is burnt down or destroyed by fire or hurricane or earthquake.

If this business had no insurance against the above three perils, two questions arise:

(a) Who would pay for such a huge loss; and

(b) Where would money come from to restart the business?

Of course if this very same business had had insurance for public liability it would get nothing because public liability cover does not cover losses caused by hurricane or earthquake or fire.

Now, just as an individual who is a worker feels more comfortable and assured if he or she has a sense of financial security, the owners and operators of a business and in particular the directors would sleep better each night if their businesses were protected by insurance against all foreseeable perils that could possibly disrupt their businesses operations.

General Insurance is definitely an aid or better still, part of the support system of those businesses which stand to be indemnified in the event of loss(es) caused by sudden unforeseen events.

RESEARCH TASKS

1. Find out what a cover note is.

2. How does an annuity differ from an endowment policy?

3. Distinguish between an assessor (a claims adjuster) and an actuary.

4. Find out about policies known as Life Savers or Universal policies.

QUESTIONS

1   How does an assessor (claims adjuster) differ from an actuary?

2   What does insurance coverage against public liability really entail?

3   How can an Insurance Company still make a profit even after paying out large sums of money as claims?

4   Fully explain the term insurable interest.

CHAPTER 18

BUSINESS DOCUMENTS

A business document is some record or proof of a business transaction, 'deal' or matter pointing to a business relationship.

PURPOSE OF BUSINESS DOCUMENTS

1. They are records of agreements, debt, credits and business and commercial issues.
2. They present permanent evidence or proof and can therefore be the 'memory' of contracts that have taken place.
3. They point to bundles of information which is critical to business.
4. They verify business transactions.
5. Under certain laws, particular papers, records and occurrences have to be kept in writing, often for Government to be satisfied that the country's laws have been observed.
6. Business documents provide sources of information and explain particular issues clearly.
7. For purposes of auditing and double/cross checking, business documents play a most important role.

Various business documents exist in the real world but only the more popular ones will be treated in this text.

There are documents used in the home trade and others used in the import – export business. Some documents that are commonly exploited in the home trade are also used in international trade.

SOME DOCUMENTS USED IN THE HOME TRADE

1. Letter of Enquiry
2. Quotations
3. Orders
4. Pro Forma Invoice
5. Ordinary Invoice
6. Credit Notes
7. Debit Notes
8. Statements of Account

LETTER OF ENQUIRY

Much as it is true that some shoppers including suppliers resort to telephone calls, faxes and the internet when seeking to make orders, the letter of enquiry remains an important instrument by which contact is made with suppliers to ascertain important information.

The letter of enquiry seeks information on –

> (a) The availability of goods.
> (b) The price of goods
> (c) Issues of Transport costs.
> (d) Related issues of packing and storing.

In anticipation of the type of information sought by buyers and consumers, some suppliers have available standardized forms that provide space to be filled in by the inquiring individuals.

THE QUOTATION

In answer to the buyer or consumer, the supplier provides a quotation. This sets out the terms of trade and the minimum quantities to be sold, price, handling and storage cost(s) and other things to do with the proposed sale and purchase.

THE ORDER

After the quotation has been delivered to the intended purchaser, the purchaser has time to reflect and to decide exactly what he or she will take.

An order coming from a buyer or consumer refers to:

> (a) Quantity of goods to be bought.
> (b) Where the goods are to be delivered.
> (c) Date of delivery (the date of delivery is sometimes so important when goods are needed urgently, that many a buyer informs the seller that time is of essence).
> (d) If the suppliers meet the cost of transport and related matters.
> (e) The price to be paid by the buyer (consumer).

It is a regular custom for suppliers to indicate that they have received the order by confirming that the order has been received and when he or she is ready to deliver the order.

THE PRO FORMA INVOICE

Where the supplier has never dealt with the purchaser and is unsure about the latter's bona fides, a pro forma invoice seeking advance payment may be sent to the new buyer spelling out all the relevant particulars. Except for demanding payment 'up front' the pro forma invoice resembles ordinary invoices.

ORDINARY INVOICE

Ordinary invoices are dispatched from the seller to buyer and contain information in respect of:

    (a) Quantity of goods being supplied.

    (b) A breakdown of individual unit price.

    (c) The actual amount(s) of money which are owed.

The invoice is usually numbered to aid things like recovery of records, times of delivery and such like.

THE CREDIT NOTE

It often happens that goods are delivered in short supply and that the buyer has overpaid the seller. When this happens the seller issues what is described as a Credit Note. The Credit Note is normally printed in red and seeks to reconcile differences between seller and buyer.

THE DEBIT NOTE

A buyer may end up receiving and accepting more goods than were ordered. Where the buyer accepts additional goods he or she is indebted to the seller. It may also be the case that the seller has undercharged the buyer for goods supplied. In the above two examples a Debit Note is issued with the aim of correcting the problems.

THE STATEMENT OF ACCOUNT

It often happens that within a given period dozens of transactions occur between a given seller and a particular buyer. These transactions may be so frequent that it becomes inconvenient to make payments regularly. In any event goods sent in the manner described here are sold on credit.

The Statement of Account is used for the following purposes:

    (a) When debt is already owing to the supplier this debt is communicated.

    (b) New amounts owing are listed.

When the seller himself is indebted to the buyer a 'set off' arrangement can be organized.

The Statement of Account tends to show business transactions which have taken place over time and sets out to present accurate financial information between seller and buyer.

DISCOUNTS

Discounts are rebates and reductions in prices usually to encourage more sales and turnover as between Seller and Buyer.

TRADE DISCOUNTS

Imagine a wholesaler who trades in sardines and corned beef. He sells to Joanne who is a retailer. The wholesaler offers Joanne a trade discount thereby offering lower prices than would have been the case in ordinary circumstances.

This discount serves as an incentive to Joanne 'to get on with it' and to return to the wholesaler for new and additional supplies.

QUANTITY DISCOUNT

This discount is allowed by the seller to the buyer so that the buyer can purchase huge quantities. It is a discount on huge volumes of sales.

CASH DISCOUNT

In the Wholesale and Retail Trade, accounts are usually settled within a thirty day period. So there is considerable crediting (and owing) in this type of business. Where the seller wishes to entice his clients to settle their accounts within a short time frame, a cash discount may be offered to encourage prompt or early payment and increases the cash flow of the supplier.

DOCUMENTS USED IN INTERNATIONAL TRADE

In this section attention will be focused on:-

(1) The Bill of Lading.
(2) The Air Way Bill.
(3) The Ship's Manifest.
(4) The Bill of Exchange.

THE BILL OF LADING

As far as transport of cargo by ships is concerned the Bill of Lading is an extremely important document. Firstly bear in mind that ships transport cargo on contract with exporters and this cargo has to reach a definite location.

One of the defining features of the Bill of Lading is that it is a document indicating ownership and title.

Cargo ships do not accept cargo until the ships' captains are clear about:-
(a) Identity of the Exporter.
(b) Identity of the Importer.
(c) Particulars are listed in the Bill of Lading and so far as Bills of Lading are concerned, copies of these important documents are retained by the exporter, delivered to the ship's captain, and kept for the importer's record as evidence.

THE AIR WAY BILL (Used on Aircraft)

The Air Way Bill is never a document of ownership or title but is otherwise similar to the Bill of Lading.

It serves as a kind of receipt taken by the airline so that it can be traced. On occasions it has happened that goods have been flown without any accompanying documents. Air Way Bills largely resemble Bills of Lading but their use is restricted to air transport.

THE SHIP'S MANIFEST

A Ship's Manifest is a collection of all the Bills of Lading and cargo carried on the ship. The importance of a ship's manifest does NOT only lie in the fact that it records cargo and documents relevant to cargo but for purposes of Customs' rules and regulations such are necessary.

BILLS OF EXCHANGE

Used primarily in international trade and in a limited way in the home trade, A Bill of Exchange, vouching for payment, is issued by the creditor or exporter or seller of goods and services requiring payment by a given date.

The Bill of Exchange may require payment on demand or on some given date. The Bill of Exchange is a legal document spelling out the obligations of the parties to it. It is in widespread use in foreign trade. It is used by the seller. So long as a Bill of Exchange is in good order, its recipient can sell it to a Discount House or Factor and it will be honoured.

One of the effects of the issue of a Bill of Exchange is that its use can allow buyers and purchasers to obtain goods and services in good time thereby allowing them to conduct their trade while the issuer of the Bill is guaranteed payment.

Commercial Banks do play a role not only by facilitating these Bills but also by indicating which customers are worthy of credit.

There now follows very brief descriptions of a few matters pertinent to Business documents:

    (a) Import Licences;
    (b) Export Licences;
    (c) Certificates of Origin; and
    (d) Freight Notes.

IMPORT LICENCE

Most countries control in different ways the volume of imports entering them. Despite trade liberalization some countries insist on Import Quotas often to protect local business and to control outflows of foreign exchange.

An import licence gives permission to allow certain goods to enter the country.

EXPORT LICENCE

The idea of requiring exporters to seek permission to sell abroad appears rather odd in light of the numerous benefits to be derived from exporting. Yet some countries are reluctant to allow the 'loss' of particular items of heritage, history and such like. They require export licences. Export licences are rare.

CERTIFICATES OF ORIGIN

Some countries have doubts about the quality of goods which are imported into them. Items like fish and meat are closely controlled through the implementation of health measures.

In addition, some counties give preferential treatment to imports from very, very friendly countries.

In the above two instances importing countries will probably insist on Certificates of Origin to be sure that their import regulations are obeyed.

FREIGHT NOTES

When a shipping company agrees to transport goods abroad a contract is formed. With every valid contract consideration must move from the promisee. The promisee is here the exporter who will be hiring the ship's services for the ship to transport goods to destination.

Where a shipper has agreed to convey goods, the shipper must be paid his or her consideration. When a shipper writes up the charges for carrying the goods a freight note comes into existence.

RESEARCH TASKS

1. Find out what the relevant processes are from the time goods and commodities leave their overseas ports down to reaching their Caribbean destinations.

2. What role do the Customs play in the import and export business?

3. Research the role of a customs broker.

QUESTIONS

1   (a) What do the letters f.o.b. stand for?

    (b) What do the letters c.i.f. stand for?
2   What are discount houses?
3   Explain the importance of an import licence.
4   Explain the difference between a pro forma invoice and an ordinary invoice.

CHAPTER 19

LEGAL ASPECTS OF BUSINESS

For purposes of this Chapter consideration will be given to elements of the Law of Contract.

DEFINITION OF CONTRACT

A contract is a legally binding agreement showing an intention to create legal relations. Expressed another way a contract is an enforceable agreement in which the parties to the agreement have shown by words or by conduct that they intend to be bound by the terms and conditions to which they have consented. Most contracts are oral, but specialty contracts, contracts for the sale of land and contracts of guarantee must be in writing.

INTENTION TO BE BOUND

It has been a well-established rule that if an arrangement is so informal that there is no intention to create legal relations among the parties, there can be no contract.

So for there to be a true contract there must be proof that all parties to the contract wish both to play their part in a serious way and with a determination that their bargain be enforceable by the law courts.

FORMALITIES

Certain contracts must be in writing. Contracts of guarantee and Contracts of insurance have to be in written form. Other contracts which require utmost good faith must also be written. These include marine contracts.

SPECIALTY CONTRACTS

A specialty contract is a contract in writing and under seal. Usually no consideration beyond the seal is necessary.

ORAL CONTRACTS

Oral or parol contracts are permitted by law. Many contracts are done daily by word of mouth. When Mary buys doubles or a roti from Veejay at Curepe Junction, Trinidad and Tobago, there is a legally binding agreement which is not put into written form.

Veejay wishes to be paid for his Doubles or Roti while Mary wants a good roti fit for the purpose for which she is buying it, and their bargain is sufficiently formal and serious, for the law to uphold their agreement.

Similarly when a person goes to a restaurant and orders a meal, no time is taken writing up a contract but such a business transaction with its offer, acceptance, capacity, consideration, legality and voluntariness will point to a contract. In the real world if every single contract had to be in writing there would be enormous waste of time and business would proceed very, very slowly.

ESSENTIAL FEATURES OF CONTRACTS

Every contract, however simple or complex only comes into being after certain basic requirements of law are seen to be in place.

These are:
(1) Offer and Acceptance.
(2) Consideration.
(3) Capacity.
(4) Absence of fraud, mistake and misrepresentation.
(5) Absence of force, duress, oppression and coercion.
(6) Legality.

Before proceeding to discuss 'offer' it is necessary to consider invitation to treat and to distinguish it from offer.

Invitation to Treat

An advertisement or a signal that something is to be traded which does not show a definitive offer and is never an offer is merely an invitation to treat. This is deemed as pre-contractual. Generally pre-contractual matters do not form part of a contract. Goods in a display window, items advertised in a catalogue invite attention, but without more, do not point to an offer.

Offer

An offer is a clear indication that the person who is making it is absolutely determined to make a commodity, product or service available (to an offeree or offerees).

An offer may be made in words or by conduct. An important rule is that the person(s) to whom this offer is extended must accept it in the very terms and on the exact conditions in which it is made.

Counter-Offer

Where the person to whom an offer is made responds by requesting the offeror to change the terms of the offer, the offeree is not signaling a true acceptance. Instead the offeree is making a counter-offer which is the offeree's response asking for a variation of terms and conditions. As an offer must be accepted on the exact terms in which it is made, where the offeree asks for a change to what is being offered, there is no acceptance. Where a person makes a counter offer, the original offer ends. Therefore after making a counter offer which is rejected, the offeree cannot return to indicate that he or she wants to respond to the original offer.

However, asking for more details about an offer is never a counter-offer.

Revocation of Offer

If the offeror has made his intention to be bound by making an offer to another person (the offeree) who takes very long to respond or does not make their intention known up to the date the offer is to last, the offeror can revoke the offer. Revocation of an offer can occur at any time before acceptance is made.

Lapse of Offer

Where an offer has been made and the offeree is expected to respond with acceptance within a reasonable or agreed time and fails to do so, the offer lapses. Clearly no offer should remain open indefinitely as it would mean forcing the offeror to wait for an excessively long time.

There are instances where time is of essence as far as the offer is concerned, meaning that the terms of the proposed contract require prompt acceptance.

Acceptance

The offeree must accept the offer exactly as the offer is made. Acceptance must come within a reasonable time or by the time stated as the time for acceptance. If the offer is revoked in good time, there could be no point in attempting to accept.

Acceptance in good time will pave the way for a contract to be made **provided that all the other essential features are present in the contract.**

Finally no one can go to another and say "I accept what you have" if no genuine offer had been made. In addition if there is an attempt at acceptance and any one of the other essential features is missing there can be no binding contract.

One of the essential features is **Consideration.**

Consideration

Consideration is the price or money paid to clinch a bargain or agreement. To some persons Consideration is the promise put forward by one party (the offeree) and accepted by the other (the offeror) as the price of that other person's promise.

Consideration must move from the promisee or offeree. This means that the person who is to benefit from the performance of the contract must pay or provide something in return. Consideration must be real. This means that no fanciful thing will be good enough consideration. Consideration must be sufficient enough to clinch the deal. The law allows for persons to agree their own price even when the price is below market value. Consideration must be sufficient but need not be adequate. If the price is inadequate in terms of true market value but is sufficient in the eyes of the law, it will suffice.

Consideration must not be past. What this means is that the Consideration or price should be known before or at the time of the contract. So if John offers Abdullah a ride to the city over a drive of twelve miles without mentioning to his passenger beforehand that there is a price, John cannot come after the fact and insist that Abdullah pay!

Executory and Executed Consideration

In character Consideration is of two types. Executory Consideration and Executed Consideration. Contract law treats a promise to pay and a promise to perform as being good enough to show an intention to be bound. Therefore in the right scenario "A promise is a debt" and 'Breach of Promise' is breach of contract. If John promises to pay $200.00 for 20 pounds of beef to Ronaldo when the latter delivers the beef three weeks into the future, there is a binding contract even though no money has been paid nor beef yet delivered. Clearly this is so if Ronaldo had promised delivery at the agreed time.

Where a contract is founded on a promise or promises it is said to exist at the executory stage.

Executed Consideration

Where the price is paid or the agreed promise of the payment has been tendered, it is normal to speak of executed consideration. Executed Consideration can be taken to be consideration taken beyond a promise up to the handing over of actual payment or something of value in lieu of payment.

Capacity

Human beings who have reached the age of majority are legal persons who can enter into legal relations and can sue and be sued.

Incorporated companies, registered co-operatives with limited liability and public corporations and authorities are called legal persons, though they have no brain or heart. They are therefore artificial legal persons.

The law treats actual human beings and artificial human beings as both being able to carry legal capacity. Minors have contractual capacity to trade in things which are necessary for them.

Where a minor enters into a contract for items or commodities which are not necessary for them the minor can avoid this contract.

Where an adult sells something to a minor or contracts with a minor, the adult must prove that the contract was necessary for the minor.

Where people are drunk, drugged or insane they are not permitted to enter in binding contracts.

Misrepresentation and Mistake

There must be neither mistake nor misrepresentation strong enough to make the contract void. Some instances of mistake and misrepresentation are not that serious to negative a contract. Where a person stands to lose on account of a mistake or misrepresentation it is up to them to choose to continue with the contract or to abandon it. If they continue, the contract is very much valid, if they pull out of it, it becomes void.

No Coercion or Duress

All parties to a contract must enter it of their own free will. Someone pressured into an 'agreement' can pull out and make it void.

Void and Voidable Contracts

A void contract is no contract. The so-called agreement is so badly infected, usually by illegality, that in the eyes of the law it is not good enough to be a legal or valid contract. 'Contracts' to trade in illegal goods, of prostitution, and of law-breaking will not be upheld and are always void.

A voidable contract is one in which there are problems of misrepresentation and or mistake. With a voidable contract the party who stands to lose or to suffer on account of distortions of fact or misrepresentation and or mistake is given a choice. They can refuse to go through with the contract thereby cancelling it and making it void but if they wish to, they can affirm the contract and make it valid. E.g. Tyrone lies to Indira saying that the car he wishes to sell her for $20,000 is a 2002 model. After Indira realizes that the car is really a 1998 model she can choose to pull out of contract thereby making it void. But if she really likes the car she can affirm the contract and remain in it. To cancel it makes it void. To elect to remain in the contract is to make a valid contract.

A voidable contract is one where one of the parties has legal power to treat it as bad if they wish to or to treat it as good if they so desire. It is therefore voidable at the instance of the innocent party.

Frustration

Consider the below example:

Nedd agrees to rent Fred's shed for $300.00 on the 30th December to hold a fete. On the 28th December Ted a vagrant, falls asleep outside the shed and when he awakes he lights a fire close to the shed and the fire spreads and burns down the shed.

Here the shed is

  (a) Destroyed before the date set for performance by Fred.
  (b) Destroyed by the act of a party who is not a party to the contract.
  (c) No longer available to Nedd.

The fire has occurred in a way that is beyond the control of the parties to the contract.

Frustration of contract can be described as an act which terminates a contract after making it impossible to be performed.

When frustration occurs, it is always caused by some new, usually unforeseen act coming about to frustrate the intention of the parties. However, where a person through indiscipline or a self-induced condition is 'unable' to perform their part of the bargain there is no frustration of contract.

For there to be a frustration, something entirely beyond the control of the parties e.g. a hurricane or earthquake must 'intervene' to prevent the performance of the contract. An act of someone outside the contract can frustrate it. When a contract is terminated by frustration the parties to the contract are placed in a position where they would have been, if there was no contract at all.

BREACH OF CONTRACT

Anticipatory Breach

Consider this fact situation:

Joe tells Dean:

"If you pay me $28,000 next month I will sell you my car."

Dean says:
"I will buy your car next month for $28,000."

Before the time of the completion and close of the deal occurs, Dean telephones Joe and says

"I have changed my mind."

This is a case of anticipatory breach. It is anticipatory because there is time left before performance.

Where an anticipatory breach occurs the party who stands to lose and who clearly is not the one who is responsible for threatening the breach has a choice.

This choice is

    (a) They can sue immediately for the anticipatory breach.

    (b) They can wait until the date set for performance and when the contract breaker truly breaks the contract by not performing their part on the date of performance, the innocent party can sue for actual breach of contract.

Actual Breach

An actual breach occurs when:

1. A party fails or refuses to perform their part.
2. Through their own fault and state, the contract is not performed e.g. Jim is to transport Sally to the airport at 3.00 p.m. on 15th November. At 3.00 p.m. on 15th November after 2 ½ hrs. of non-stop drinking Jim is so drunk he gets a friend to phone Sally saying it is impossible for him to take Sally.

Here Jim is in breach by doing something to himself which made him break his promise.

1. A party performs their part so badly as to defeat the clear intention of the parties.
2. With time being of extreme importance a party 'performs' way out of time.

So long as a breach is proved, the innocent party or the one not responsible for the breach is usually entitled to damages.

METHODS BY WHICH A CONTRACT CAN BE TERMINATED

1. By performance.
2. By frustration.
3. By breach.
4. By mutual agreement.
5. Through Accord and Satisfaction.

Where the parties to a contract have played their part by meeting their obligations and all the terms and conditions, there is termination or discharge by performance.

In instances where some new or supervening act has occurred which prevents the contract from being performed there is discharge or termination by frustration.

When a contract has been agreed it is binding on the parties. If a party to a contract fails or refuses to play their part in fulfilling the terms of the contract even though it ends abruptly, it is deemed to be terminated or discharged by breach.

There are cases when one of the parties might seek to change, vary or end the contract. There can be a termination or discharge by mutual agreement.

Where the parties are bound by the terms of an existing agreement generally speaking they ought to abide by what they have agreed.

However upon the payment of fresh or new consideration (satisfaction) the parties can create an entirely new agreement to replace the original one. The new agreement supported by satisfaction is said to be reached by accord.

'Satisfaction' means consideration in this context.

RESEARCH TASKS

1. Find out what misrepresentation means.

2. Ascertain whether outside of money, consideration can mean or refer to other things.

3. What is the legal definition of capacity?

4. What is revocation and what effect does revocation have?

5. How does lapse of offer differ from an anticipatory breach?

QUESTIONS

1 Explain the meaning of contractual capacity.

2 How does frustration differ from breach?

3 What is a specialty contract?

4 Distinguish between a void and voidable contract.

CHAPTER 20

GOVERNMENT

DEFINITION

Government may be defined as that national institution which is responsible for the regulation, control and management of the country in which it is established.

Every country on earth has a Government though in some unfortunate parts of the world there are cases of different groups simultaneously claiming to be the Government of the place for which they are vying.

BASIC FUNCTIONS AND PURPOSE OF GOVERNMENT

1. To provide security to their citizens through Police Services, Fire Services, Defence Forces and armies.
2. To pass laws to modernize how Government departments function.
3. To provide hospitals and health care.
4. To provide opportunities for education and training.
5. To provide basic consumer protection through consumer protection laws.

Governments are associated with the tasks of providing health care and this explains why many Caribbean countries offer free health care in hospitals, clinics and polyclinics.

Government also offers protection through social security benefits and pensions. Examples of benefits are sickness benefits, employment, injury and maternity benefits, contributory pensions and financial grants.

Non-contributory pensions for the elderly are also provided. In some Caribbean countries Social Security which is a form of compulsory insurance for workers, is known as National Insurance.

Schools, learning institutions and training organizations are either provided by Governments directly or are facilitated by Governments.

Finally infrastructure such as roads, ports, bridges and transportation are made available by Caribbean governments. Such tend to be costly and in many instances the Caribbean Development Bank and the Inter-American Bank have assisted with funding infrastructure

HIGHER FUNCTIONS OF GOVERNMENT

1. To facilitate the development and growth of commerce, business and industry.
2. To ensure that commercial activity is at a level that satisfies the community.

3. To manage the economy by ensuring that Central Banks undertake measures to ensure the sound health of the economy.
4. To pass laws that do not only protect society at the level of national security but also by ensuring that there are rules and policies which facilitate the business sector.
5. To negotiate with foreign governments in the interest of better and smoother bilateral and multilateral trade and commercial agreements.
6. To work with international organizations which could provide things like technical support and financial assistance.
7. To establish and run institutions like Court Registries, Central Banks , Land Registries, Customs Departments etc. for the betterment of the country.

GOVERNMENT'S ROLE IN THE ECONOMY

Caribbean governments do not practice laissez-faire but play an active role in the economy. Government's role in the National Economy (considering the role of the Central Bank and the Treasury and the Inland Revenue Departments), shows that Government works through specific institutions to achieve objectives like the formulation and execution of monetary and fiscal policies.

Through Institutions like Companies Registries and the Registry responsible for Co-operatives, Government puts policies and programmes in place to offer direction to companies and co-operatives and other institutions.

In addition:

- Through its Ministry of Finance, Planning and Economic Affairs.
- Through its Ministry of Trade and Commerce.
- Through its Ministry of International Business.
- Through its Ministry of Industry and Manufacturing
- Through its Ministry of Lands, Mining and Natural Resources
- Through its Ministry of Tourism   among others,

Government provides support and resources for programmes designed to bring about economic development and growth.

GOVERNMENT AND TAXATION

All Caribbean governments, like others abroad, must have money to finance their projects and activities, plant, equipment and certain running costs like the payment of salaries and wages for public sector employees such as civil servants and employees of State-run Associations, Corporations and Statutory Boards.

For Governments to be able to meet their expenditure they must extract money from some source. Government extracts money from various sources.

Most of the money which goes into the Treasuries of Government is raised by the imposition of Taxation.

TAXATION

A tax is a sum of money raised by Government by means of a legal process which requires individuals, firms and companies to pay over particular amounts to the Government Treasury.

In addition a tax is a financial imposition and where various sectors have to pay tax by law, they are under an obligation to do so. Taxes are labelled as Direct Taxes or Indirect Taxes.

DIRECT TAXES

Where Government takes part of the earnings of a company via corporation tax, such a tax is directly imposed on the corporation and cannot be shifted off the corporation. Similarly where citizens are compelled by law to part with a percentage of their wages and salaries which Government collects and puts into its Revenue, these citizens are paying their (income) taxes directly. Income Tax, also known as P.A.Y.E. (Pay as You Earn) is another example of a Direct Tax. Land Tax is also a direct tax.

There also exist levies which are kinds of taxes aimed for specific purposes. Some of the levies are imposed on areas like transportation, the environment and training. When these purposes are fulfilled, the levies are dropped.

INDIRECT TAXATION

The most obvious characteristic of an Indirect Tax is that it can be shifted by the firm or entity on which it was originally imposed and made payable by someone else.

Examples of Indirect Taxes are Value Added Tax, consumption taxes and Import and Customs Duties.

Excise taxes which are also indirect in nature, are imposed on spirits and fuels.

Where taxation policy requires the rich to pay a greater proportion of their earnings than is paid by less well-off persons, one speaks of a progressive tax policy.

Where however the poor must pay a greater proportion of their income and earnings than do the rich, a regressive tax policy is said to exist.

A proportional tax is one which sees a fixed portion of tax extracted by Government.

Consider the below examples.

> Rasheed earns $2,000 per month and has to pay $200.00 in PAYE.
> Erla earns $1,000 per month and has to pay $100.00 in taxes (PAYE).

In the above examples Rasheed and Erla pay a fixed portion of 10% on their income.
A proportional tax, unlike a regressive or progressive tax, is one where a predictable and known portion of tax is taken out by Government.

Such a type of tax is often deemed fair especially by those who oppose progressive tax systems.

With a progressive tax system the more one earns the more one pays in taxes. Naturally the awkward regressive tax system actually requires the poor to pay more taxes or a greater proportion of taxes than the better-off elements in the community.

GOVERNMENTS AND FISCAL POLICY

Consider the below:

Government recently announced a 10% increase in all taxes right across the board. This includes income tax or PAYE.

The question arises as to why would Government take such a serious step.

If it is taken that Government is worried that consumption is too high thereby leading to excessive demand especially of imported goods, then it can be argued that Government is using an increase in taxation to slow down demand and so export less foreign exchange.

If it is taken that Government is very short on money then the increase in taxation is here prompted by the need for Government to raise additional revenue. However sharp, sudden increases in taxes always cause the population to be alarmed. The question is always why an increase in taxes?

Even when Government needs to raise additional revenue it must be indicated that taxation is always seen as a burden to lowly paid wage-earners and a disincentive to business activity.

Heavy taxes on commercial institutions can

1. Cause production to fall.
2. Cause business people to retrench workers.
3. Lead some business people to take money overseas out of the economy.

4. Cause a decrease in investor confidence.
5. Discourage existing businesses from expansion.
6. Encourage new businesses to postpone investment or locate elsewhere.
7. Ultimately lead to a decline in economic activity and growth.

EFFECT OF DECREASE IN TAXATION

Much as Government always needs revenue it must be alert to the fact that tax concessions are usually welcome both by business people and consumers.

A reduction in taxes on businesses can -
   i. Increase the income of businesses.
   ii. Encourage some businesses to put money in expansion and further investment.
   iii. Encourage businesses to employ more workers.
   iv. Encourage businesses to increase wages and salaries.
   v. Motivate the productive sectors to produce more.
   vi. Inspire wage-earners and consumers to save more.
   vii. Inspire wage-earners and consumers to purchase more household and other items.
   viii. Inspire greater productivity among the workforce.
   ix. Lead to an increase in overall economic activity and growth.

Attention will now be paid to the Common External Tariff (C.E.T.)

THE COMMON EXTERNAL TARIFF

Within Caricom there is no tariff on local goods traded between Caricom territories.

However there is a tariff imposed on certain classes of goods that are imported from outside Caricom.

Briefly the Common External Tariff (C.E.T.) is imposed by Caricom on foreign goods which enter Caricom in competition against Caricom produced goods.

The Common External Tariff is designed to make foreign goods more expensive than Caricom produced goods.

If foreign goods are cheaper than local goods, competition becomes an issue in which local goods will be traded at a disadvantage in the local market.

Recently the Common External Tariff in some Caribbean countries has been reduced to lower the cost of living on account of the sharp increases in the prices of food and energy.

RESEARCH TASKS

1. Gather information on the general system of Government in three Caribbean territories.

2. Explore how the behaviour and policies of a government can cause economic hardship. Provide examples.

3. Carefully research the rationale behind C.E.T.

4. Research what a Common Market entails.

5. Select four Government departments and show how they contribute to commercial and economic programmes and policies.

QUESTIONS

1   Identify three ways in which Caribbean governments have used fiscal measures to assist business development.

2   Where taxation is seen as too high, explain two ways in which businesses are negatively affected.

3   How does taxation affect the average consumer?

CHAPTER 21

SOCIAL ACCOUNTING

In this chapter concepts such as quality of life of citizens, a country's standard of living and measures of a country's earnings are considered among other things.

A COUNTRY'S STANDARD OF LIVING

Many writers have tended to consider a country's standard of living within a macro economic framework. This approach treats to the issue of the state of the overall wealth and progress of a given country but ignores the plight of individual residents.

Six variables can be considered as pointing to a country's overall wealth. These are:

(i)   the level and quantity of consumption of products and services;
(ii)   the disposable income of the population as a whole;
(iii)   the presence of capital equipment which is made use of in the country;
(iv)   the availability of modern equipment, technology and automatic machinery;
(v)   the amount of investment in research and technology;
(vi)   The reputation of the country in the eyes of the international community.

The six indices above will point to the state of the country as a whole but do not give enough information as to the quality of life of the many individuals who live in the country.

COST OF LIVING

The cost of living refers to what it takes for persons to purchase food, garments and personal effects. It is related to the general level of prices within a particular economy. Where prices continue to rise it is normal to speak of increases in inflation. However, for inflation to be an issue there must be a persistent increase in the general level of prices and where the increases cannot be controlled one can speak of run-away inflation or galloping inflation.

Readers are cautioned, however, never to confuse the concept of standard of living with that of cost of living though it is certain that where the cost of living is out of control it will impact on the standard of living especially since it would erode disposable incomes.

THE QUALITY OF LIFE OF INDIVIDUALS IN THE POPULATION

In a very real sense a country's population depends on the resources which are made available to the people at large. Quite often, indeed on a regular basis, the resources of Caribbean countries are increased through imports.

In assessing the quality of life of a population, the below factors have to be taken into account:

(i) the availability, cost and quality of food;

(ii) the degree to which the people in the country enjoy a high level of personal security against crime and violence;

(iii) the availability of schooling and training opportunities.

(iv) the extent to which there are significant rates of infant mortality;

(v) the availability to individuals of running water, electricity and telephone services.

(vi) levels of employment.

NATIONAL INCOME

National Income which is very closely related to a country's Gross Domestic Product refers to the 'earnings' of a country within a given period, usually a year.

A country's Gross Domestic Product is the value in money of the internal earnings of a country measured with a given period.

Most territories measure their National Income and Gross Domestic Product with reference to a year.

The distinction between Gross Domestic Product and the Gross National product will be examined later in this chapter.

HOW NATIONAL INCOME IS MEASURED

There are three ways of measuring the National Income and these are:

1. The Output Approach;
2. The Income Approach; and
3. The Expenditure Approach.

THE OUTPUT APPROACH

The output method refers to the value of all goods and services produced in the economy after depreciation is deducted from the gross amount or overall figure. In essence the output method takes into account the value of total production but makes allowance for the amount of wear and tear recorded to take into account the extent to which machinery, equipment and buildings have lost some of their value on account of depreciation.

The output method or approach therefore points to the net output or true value of total production.

Where particular goods go through stages from primary production to the secondary stage there is the possibility that these goods may be accounted for twice so one of the challenges of the output approach is to avoid counting the same goods and services twice.

THE INCOME APPROACH

One way of finding a monetary measure of a country's periodic (usually a year) performance is to add together all wages, salaries, profits and rents recorded in the period.

When all these earnings are totaled up, the total or aggregate of all money earned is arrived at.

The Income Approach therefore totals the monetary earnings of a country and the total figure arrived at, should be the same as the figure from the net output of the economy.

THE EXPENDITURE APPROACH

In every economy spending occurs both daily and also over a period of time. Without considering patterns of spending or trends in aggregate national demand, it can still be said that when the value of all consumer spending, spending by government and spending by firms and businesses is added together, the result in monetary terms ought to be the same figure as was arrived at from the Output Approach and indeed for the Income Approach as well.

GROSS DOMESTIC PRODUCT

The Gross Domestic Product refers to the income earned in any economy in a given period usually a year.

Many economists use Gross Domestic Product and National Income interchangeably.

GROSS NATIONAL PRODUCT

The gross national product can best be defined as the total monetary value produced by all nationals of a given country or economy. Many American citizens own businesses located outside of America and remit income and profits back to their home country.

For example if some 1,000 American businesses operating offshore sent back money to the U.S.A. such earnings counted up, are added to America's Gross Domestic Product to arrive at the Gross National Product.

As observed above Caribbean countries tend to use Gross Domestic Product in their countries measurement simply because of a situation where the nationals of individual Caribbean countries do not as a rule send back incomes and profits because offshore Caribbean businesses exist in such few numbers that remittances sent back by Caribbean people are so negligible as not to affect the National Income of individual Caribbean countries in any significant way.

PER CAPITA INCOME

If the term per capita income is taken literally it means earnings per head (of the population). Much attention has been paid to per capita income as an economic indicator but in practice it has its limitations. The per capita income is arrived at by dividing the National Income by the total population.

If a country boasts of a per capita income of $15,000 (fifteen thousand dollars) at first the impression could be conveyed that the average person has an opportunity to earn this amount of money.

In practice though, those income earning units that have incomes way in excess of $15,000 will be responsible for raising the per capita income while most persons do not earn so much.

Study the below table which applies to a country with a National Income of about 850,000 000 million and a population of 85,000 and a per capita income of $10,000

INCOME	PERCENTAGE OF POPULATION
125,999 and above	6
100,000 - 125,000	8
75,000 - 100,000	12
65,000 - 75,000	6
3,000 - 4,000	68

One of the more obvious shortcomings of per capita income is that it does not show how income is distributed.

A country can have an impressive per capita income while the majority of people in the country live in poverty.

Per capita income as a measure of a country's wealth does not point to
  (a) number of persons with access to decent housing;
  (b) number of persons who can access decent health care;
  (c) the level of the country's overall level of development;
  (d) how any growth in the economy impacts on all segments of society;
  (e) per capita income can on many occasions signal growth and an increase in the earnings of the country without indicating how income is really distributed.

GROWTH AND DEVELOPMENT

Growth refers to a measurable method of calculating whether a country's national income has decreased or increased. When the National Income has decreased there is said to be negative growth. However, when the size of the national income has grown or increased, positive growth has occurred.

Economic growth points to a measurable performance and never points to the true level of development of a given country. For example, a country can experience positive growth and still have poor health care, inadequate housing, run-down schools or insufficient schools and high levels of unemployment. Development on the other hand is more to do with the state and condition of a country at a given period of time. Development will concern itself with things like availability of drinking water, presence of electricity and other utilities, life expectancy, availability of health, educational and recreational facilities, levels of income and employment, presence and use of technology and the level of consumption of goods and services. Where the above things abound there will be development and the presence of these things in abundance could occur even when there is negative growth in the economy.

THE ROLE OF HUMAN RESOURCE DEVELOPMENT

Human Resource Development is concerned with the education, training and preparation of a country's population to equip them to function in the job market and to contribute to national development. In many instances, Human Resource Development goes beyond the formal academic training for which Caribbean educational systems are known. One of the key features of Human Resource Development is to so prepare participants in training, instruction and education as to equip them to function effectively and efficiently in the workplace. In some measure though, National Vocational qualifications and the method by which these qualifications are earned, actually permit people to take part in on-the-job training.

Human Resource Development is aimed at bringing the best out of workers and participants on the labour market. Its ultimate aim is to ensure the highest possible levels of productivity.

Where people are uneducated and untrained and lack skills they would definitely not be able to contribute much to national development and growth.

HUMAN RESOURCE DEVELOPMENT CONTRIBUTION TO IMPORTANT NATIONAL GOALS AND INITIATIVES

Where people are properly trained and educated and have the correct attitude to work the following benefits can occur:
  (i)   tasks are done on time;
  (ii)   work is performed with the requisite expertise.
  (iii) managers can delegate to subordinates without having to worry;
  (iv)   succession planning at an enterprise can be done fearlessly;
  (v)   some worker attitudes lead to savings but above all properly trained manpower can lead
          to very high levels of work and labour productivity.

Attention is now focused in this Chapter on International Trade.

REASONS FOR INTERNATIONAL TRADE

Where a country produces goods and services in surplus it can export the surplus and earn foreign exchange. Where a country has developed enormous expertise in the production and manufacture of particular goods and services then it can export these goods and services and earn foreign exchange. Trading and selling abroad by exporting surplus, reduces the problem of over-production.

REASONS FOR THE IMPORT TRADE

Where the local territory does not produce goods it has to buy these goods from foreign countries by means of imports.

Caribbean countries experience scarcities to such an extent that many a Caribbean country imports in excess of 70% of the goods and services consumed in the local territory. Large developed countries have for many reasons developed important technologies which either cannot be produced in the Caribbean or will have to be manufactured at tremendous monetary cost. It therefore follows that Caribbean countries have to import.

INVISIBLE IMPORTS AND EXPORTS

Where banks, insurance companies, ships and air services perform services for Caribbean countries and are paid in foreign exchange, the Caribbean is said to be importing these services.

Imports of these services are paid for in foreign exchange. To the extent that they are paid for in foreign exchange they stand in the same position as solid imported goods.

Where Caribbean banks, insurance companies, ships, aircraft and those involved in tourism perform services for non-Caribbean nations and Caribbean nations are paid in foreign exchange, this scenario is one like where the Caribbean is selling (by export) something overseas and paid in foreign exchange in return.

Increasingly the Caribbean region is selling more and more services abroad.

The best known service which is provided in the Caribbean is tourism.

Trade in services is called Invisible Trade.

BALANCE OF TRADE

Consider the scenario below:

Country F trades with Country G. At the end of the year it is realized that Country G has bought $2m in goods from Country F which in turn sold $4m in goods to Country G. This case shows that the trade between Country F and G favours Country F and so Country F has a favourable Balance of trade with Country G which can be said to have an unfavourable Balance of trade with Country F.

Balance of Trade is the end result of the export/import ratios either between two trading partners or the idea can be applied across the board to look at the difference in sales that may exist between different sets or groups of trading partners.

BALANCE OF PAYMENTS

Linked to the concept of Balance of Trade is the idea of the Balance of Payments.

Consider the following example:

At the end of a given trading year, for example, the year 2015 it has been realized that Country A has imported 3 billion in goods from other countries while exporting just $750,000 in goods.

In monetary terms Country A can be said to be in debt and to have an unfavourable Balance of Payments situation.

In the above example it was shown that Country A has a Balance of Payments deficit meaning that there is an enormous monetary gap between what a country earns and what it has to pay out. Many a Caribbean country has had Balance of Payment problems.

Linked to the Balance of Payment situation is the national debt of given country and the budgets of many a Caribbean country have shown that some Governments actually spend more in a year than they earn in taxation. Where the taxes taken in as revenue are lower than total Government spending in a period a fiscal deficit arises and indeed the country is in debt.

When there is net inflow of capital – in excess of outflows there is a favourable balance of payments situation.

It can be said in passing that the typical Caribbean country would fund its debt and fiscal deficit more so by borrowing locally and abroad than by taking in new or increased taxes.

TACKLING THE BALANCE OF PAYMENTS PROBLEM

Where a country has a Balance of Payments problem and a large fiscal deficit, it is often the case that much of the problem really arises from having to pay for an exceedingly high amount of imports while not gaining enough from exports.

Imports have to be paid for in foreign exchange and where a country has a Balance of Payments problem it almost always has a problem of insufficient current foreign funds to meet its obligations. Governments have been driven to doing some or all of the below in an effort to restrict imports and save foreign exchange.

For example, some countries have imposed tariffs on imports intending to make these imports more expensive so that the cost of imports would dissuade persons from buying such imports. Some countries have imposed import licences to restrict a number of foreign goods coming into the country. It has been the Caribbean experience in the last thirty-five or forty years for some territories to develop quotas meaning that up to a certain amount and not beyond would be the limit of imported goods that could lawfully enter the country.

To curb high importation, to deal with the question of too many imports being bought in the local territory Caribbean governments have over the years sometimes required the commercial banks to limit the amount of foreign exchange sold by these commercial banks for the importation of goods.

Jamaica, Guyana and Trinidad and Tobago have had devaluations. The purpose of devaluation at least in theory is to make imports more expensive. The expectation is that the more expensive the imports the fewer of them would be demanded and consumed. An accompanying theory is that devaluation can stimulate the demand for a territory's exports by making these exports cheaper. The reality is though that Caribbean economies have never found it easy to increase either the amount or range of their export, so devaluation has seen no widespread increases in the sales of Caribbean exports.

Another way of dealing with a shortage of foreign exchange caused by Balance of Payments problem is by barter.

For example, years ago Guyana shipped rice to Yugoslavia in exchange for tractors and it has also happened that Guyana once traded rice with Dominica in exchange for soaps made and produced in Dominica.

Finally, where a country has extremely serious Balance of Payments problems it can go to the International Monetary Fund (IMF) as the international lender of last resort. Borrowing from the IMF has proved very painful especially to Guyana and Jamaica which have experienced problems caused by the conditions on which the IMF lent money to these two territories.

The IMF almost always insists on devaluations as a condition for support provided by this agency. Devaluations have eroded the value of currencies while leading to remarkably high levels of inflation.

RESEARCH TASK

1 Research the Gross Domestic Product of five countries in the Caribbean.
2 Examine the fiscal deficit of five Caribbean countries and analyse the significance of the respective deficits

QUESTIONS

1. Explain the term standard of living.
2. Why is per capita income not the best indicator of the quality of life of citizens?
3. Differentiate between Gross Domestic Product and Gross National Product.
4. Why should a country do its utmost to develop its human resources?
5. Explain:
   (a)   Trade Balance.
   (b)   Favourable Balance of Trade.
   (c)   Balance of Payments.

CHAPTER 22

CARICOM AND THE CSME

INTRODUCTION

CARICOM means the Caribbean Community and CSME stands for Caribbean Single Market and Economy.

Between 1965 and 1968 the Governments of Antigua and Barbuda, Barbados and Guyana agreed to the formation of a Caribbean Free Trade Area (CARIFTA).

The intention was to establish a free trade area and ultimately a more heightened form of regional co-operation and integration.

The idea that the (English Speaking) Caribbean should move towards deeper integration spread and by 1970 a few other Caribbean countries joined CARIFTA.

On 4th July, 1973 at Chaguaramas a Treaty was signed by which Caricom (The Caribbean Community) was formally launched. This Treaty was signed by Jamaica, Trinidad and Tobago, Guyana and Barbados which then became known as More Developed Countries (MDC's).

When other Caribbean territories followed suit and joined not only did the numbers of Caricom countries increase but except for the four (4) founding countries all other countries were originally labelled Less Developed Countries (LDC's). To date the efforts at achieving integration have seen

   (a) Carifta
   (b) Caricom and the Common Market; and
   (c) Caricom including the CSME.

Initially known as LDCs (Less Developed Countries) such countries are now known as Disadvantaged Regions but Guyana is now treated as a Disadvantaged State.

MISSION STATEMENT OF CARICOM

"To provide dynamic leadership and service in partnership with Community institutions and groups, towards the attainment of a viable internationally competitive and sustainable community, with improve quality of life for all."

GENERAL

Objectives of CARICOM

1. To improve standards of living and work.
2. To set out to achieve full employment.
3. To exploit the non-human resources of the Caribbean region for the benefit of Caribbean peoples.
4. To achieve accelerated co-ordinated and sustained economic development.
5. To expand trading and economic relations with states outside of the Caricom region.
6. To achieve enhanced levels of international competitiveness.
7. To engender higher productivity and increased production.
8. To achieve a greater measure of economic leverage and effectiveness of member states in dealing with third party states.
9. To speak with one voice in international fora.
10. To foster enhanced co-ordination of Member States' foreign policies, especially economic policies.
11. To bring about improved functional co-operation through:
12. More efficient operation of common services, programmes, activities and policies for the benefit of those who populate Caricom countries.
13. Accelerated promotion of greater understanding among its peoples and the advancement of their economic, social, cultural and technological development.
14. Attaining intensified activities in various areas including health, education, transportation, regional security and telecommunications.

FUNCTIONS OF THE HEADQUARTERS AND SECRETARIAT OF CARICOM

1. To service meetings of the Organs of the Community and carry through with follow-up action on decisions emerging from such meetings.
2. To initiate, organize and conduct studies on issues for the attainment of the purposes of the Community.
3. To provide, on request, services to Member States of the Community on matters relating to the achievement of its objectives.
4. To collect, store and circulate to member countries of the community, information relevant for the achievement of objectives of the Community.
5. To assist in the planning and organization of sub-entities like COTED, COHSOD, COFCOR, COFAP by facilitating the programmes and activities of these units.
6. To assist community organizations in the development and implementation of proposals and programmes for the achievement of objectives of the Community.
7. To provide, when requested, technical support to national authorities to facilitate the implementation of Community decision.
8. To conduct where necessary fact finding assignments in Member States.

9. To initiate and develop proposals for consideration and decision by competent organizations in order to achieve objectives of the Community.

FUNCTIONAL AREAS

Much of the work of the Caribbean integration is undertaken by specific Institutions and Associate Institutions.

IMPORTANT CARIBBEAN INSTITUTIONS

- Caribbean Disaster Emergency Response Agency
- The Caribbean Meteorological Institute
- The Caribbean Meteorological Organization
- The Caribbean Food Corporation
- The Caribbean Environmental Health Institute
- The Caribbean Agricultural Research and Development Institute (CARDI)
- Association of Caribbean Community Parliamentarians
- Caribbean Centre for Development Administration (CARICAD)
- The Caribbean Food and Nutrition Institute.
- CARICOM Regional Organization for Standards and Quality (CROSQ).

ASSOCIATE INSTITUTIONS

- Caribbean Development Bank (CDB)
- Organisation of East Caribbean States (OECS)
- Caribbean Law Institute/Caribbean Law Institutional Centre (CLI/CLIC)
- University of Guyana (UG)
- University of the West Indies (UWI)

FREE MOVEMENT OF WORKERS AND SKILLS

The Revised Treaty of Chaguaramas allows for specific categories of workers to travel within the Caricom community to practice their professions.

Those who currently qualify to 'move freely' are
   (a) University Graduates.
   (b) Sports persons.
   (c) Journalists and Media Workers.
   (d) Artistes.
   (e) Musicians.

Such persons can make use of opportunities to gain and share professional experiences outside of their countries of original residence.

Where it is taken that these categories would wish to take their families with them the question arises as to what contingent rights they are to have.

For example, Ramnaresh travels outside of the country where he is usually resident as a citizen, and moves to Antigua and Barbuda as a sportsman.

He is contracted as a cricket coach and his wife and children have joined him.

In issue are:

(a) Will Antigua's schools permit Mrs. Ramnaresh, as wife to teach in circumstances where she is an excellent kindergarten teacher but is not a University Graduate.
(b) Can the rest of his family freely access hospital services?

The question therefore is will Caricom and the CSME allow contingent rights to the Ramnaresh family?

This matter has yet to be resolved.

HOW THE CSME IS INTENDED TO WORK

The CSME is mandated to find mechanisms to promote free trade in the region, meaning that it should not allow quantitative restrictions on the movement of goods and services nor use any methods by which free trade is impeded nor should regionally produced goods and services face (unfair) competition from extra-regional imports as far as the movement of goods is concerned.

A common external tariff (CET) of up to 40% was introduced to make non-regionally produced goods so expensive that they would not out compete local goods in the various Caricom territories.

The C.E.T. has therefore been one of the planks on which trade within Caricom has been facilitated.

Other ways by which intra-regional free trade has been encouraged is by means of the operation of Rules of Origin and restricting internal taxes on goods originating in Caricom.

Goods qualify as being of Community Origin when

(a) They are wholly produced in the Caricom Region.
(b) They are wholly or partly produced from materials imported from outside the Region or from materials of undetermined origin by a process, the effect of which is a sustainable transformation characterized by the good being classified in a tariff heading different from those goods wholly produced in the region.

The CSME exists to promote trade in services, free movement of labour and free movement of capital as well. Rights of establishment are also included and are relevant to free movement of capital.

FREE MOVEMENT OF CAPITAL AND RIGHTS OF ESTABLISHMENT

This entails member states allowing for flows of capital to move within and across the common market without hindrances or restrictions.

If business activity is to be enhanced in the Caribbean community and the CSME, then Caribbean nationals and enterprises have to be permitted to invest in member states.

The process of the movement of capital is to be facilitated by:-

(a) Ease of entry to establish a commercial presence and indefinite stay to do so.
(b) Ease of administration for the registering and/incorporation of companies and the formation of commercial firms.
(c) Access to capital in the receiving member state.
(d) Access to land, buildings and other property for purposes directly related to the establishment of a business.
(e) Freedom of entry for managerial supervisory and technical staff and spouses and immediate dependent family members.
(f) Rights of establishment point to allowing for businesses to be set up beyond their own borders.

Of note self-employed individuals who can present evidence of their bona fides are to be permitted to enter and work in states other than their original countries of residence.

A business established in one Member State under right(s) of establishment is entitled to apply for temporary or long stay in another member state for its managerial, technical and supervisory personnel.

Rights of self-employment in commercial, industrial, agricultural, professional and artisan trades are granted to create and manage business organizations engaged in the production of or trade in goods or the provision of services.

FREE MOVEMENT OF SERVICES

As far as services go where Caricom Nationals wish to trade in services they are to be accorded Most Favoured Nation treatment.

A service can be traded by means of

1. Cross Border.

2.   Consumption Abroad.
3.   Commercial Presence.
4.   Movement of Natural Persons.

As its name suggests Cross Border trade involves trade and commerce beyond and across borders.

For example, if an entity in Belize (using electronic means) conducts trade with Barbados for the mutual benefit of these two countries, there is cross border trade. This trade often involves E-commerce, contact by satellite and such like.

There is cross border trade among the stock exchanges of Barbados, Trinidad and Jamaica.

CONSUMPTION ABROAD

Consider the example below:

Country A has a number of nineteen seater aircraft but lacks the facilities to service these aircraft. Country B has all the facilities needed to repair and service the aircraft. When the aircraft is sent to Country B for maintenance consumption abroad has taken place. Country A would be 'consuming services' for Country B.

Such consumption abroad will in time gather momentum.

COMMERCIAL PRESENCE

Imagine a huge firm, Firm C which has branches and divisions in different states within the region.

Where this firm establishes offices or plants outside of its headquarter country an expansion of economic activity not only occurs but a commercial presence has been established beyond the shores of the state in which Firm C was first located.

FREE MOVEMENT OF GOODS

Goods are to be traded without restrictions.
Goods are classified as regionally produced products where:

(a) They arc wholly produced in the Caricom Community.
(b) They are wholly or partly produced from materials imported from outside the Region or from materials of undetermined origin by a process, the effect of which is a substantial transformation characterized by the good(s) being classified in a different tariff heading.

Before proceeding it must be said that up until recently integration movements worldwide commenced their initiatives by starting with free trade especially in goods and visible products.

In the past two decades globalization and trade liberalization have been proceeding rapidly.

Inevitably free trade and trade liberalization have been confronting the Caribbean.

Considering the decision taken 1989 at Grand Anse, Grenada, the Movement towards a Caribbean Single Market and Economy and all it entails is very much Caricom's regional response to globalization and trade liberalization.

RESOLVING DISPUTES

In the world of commerce and trade, trading partners often have differences, some serious, which end up as disputes.

Chapter nine of the Revised Treaty of Chaguaramas provides measures by which disputes may be resolved.

Disputes may arise in the following instances:

Where there are

(a) Allegations that the policies of member states are inconsistent with the aims of Caricom.
(b) Allegations of injury, serious prejudice encountered and or nullification or impairment of benefits expected from the Caribbean Single Market and Economy (CSME).
(c) Allegations that an organ or body within Caricom has acted outside of its legal power(s) or authority.
(d) Allegations that the purpose or object of the Treaty is being frustrated.

Under the Revised Treaty of Chaguaramas when disputes arise affected member states ought to notify the Secretary General and ideally propose to the Secretary General what manner of settlement will be used and proceed to an expeditious settlement of the disputes.

Where there are disputes, member states may request the Secretary General to use his GOOD OFFICES to solve the problem(s).

SPECIFIC MODES OF HANDLING DISPUTES

Among the other approved measures of resolving conflict in Caricom and the CSME are

1. Conciliation.
2. Mediation.
3. Consultations.
4. Arbitration and Adjudication.

CONCILIATION

A Conciliation Commission made up of three (3) persons with one conciliator appointed by each of the two parties and a third person may be established to deal with the dispute.

MEDIATION

This involves using the services of one person who is given authority to assist in resolving the dispute.

CONSULTATION

When one member state claims that actions taken by another member state are in breach of the provisions and obligations of the Treaty and has requested consultations with that other member state, that other member state is under a duty to enter into consultations with the first member state. When consultations fail the next step is Arbitration and Adjudication.

Arbitration involves making use of a forensic arbitrator while adjudication involves using a court.

The Caribbean Court of Justice has an original jurisdiction in respect of matters relevant to the interpretation of the Treaty.

Of note a member state which is NOT a party to a dispute may be allowed to attend all hearings of the arbitral tribunal and make and receive written submissions to the arbitral tribunal. Of note such a member state shall be entitled to intervene in this way before the arbitral tribunal if it delivers a notification to the parties to the dispute and to the Secretary General. The expenses and costs associated with arbitration are borne by the parties to the dispute.

THE CARIBBEAN COURT OF JUSTICE (C.C.J.)

Established by Caricom consent in Barbados on February 14, 2001 the protocol setting up the idea of this Court was signed at Montego Bay on 4th July, 2003.

The C.C.J. presently serves Guyana and Barbados, Belize and Dominica as an Appellate Court while the majority of Caricom States continue making use of the British Privy Council.

As the final appellate Court for these jurisdictions it presides over civil, criminal and public law matters.

It also has an original jurisdiction in matters pertinent to the interpretation and application of the Treaty of Chaguaramas and a minimum of three judges can adjudicate disputes. It has, however a total of ten (10) judges on its panel.

FACTORS WHICH HAVE NEGATIVELY IMPACTED ON REGIONAL INTEGRATION IN THE CARIBBEAN

Caribbean States for the most part are separated by the seas. Many are individual islands. Over the years there have been tendencies towards insularity among Caribbean nations.

Some states despite proclaiming commitments to unity and integration in principle still place their narrow self-interests as to undermine efforts at regional co-operation.

For example in the Caribbean some states recognize Taiwan as the representative as the only "TRUE CHINA" while others accept mainland China (Red China) as the real China. There is not one voice on China.

In addition suspicions exist on the ground. These suspicions go so far that many people so cling to the sovereignty of their own countries that many Caribbean people reject both the notion of free movement of workers and rights of establishment.

The Regional Integration movement has not moved rapidly forward because some territories have not readied themselves to assume particular obligations.

Deadlines have often not been met and initiatives designed to carry forward Caricom and the CSME have often been frustrated.

Caricom through its Heads of Government agreed to establish an Association of Caribbean Community Parliamentarians but precious little – indeed nothing has come out of this 'initiative'.

An entity known as the Association of Caribbean States was launched but has achieved little. In any event with Caricom and the CSME intended to be the principal organs of integration the questions arise as to whether the Association of Caribbean Community Parliamentarians and the Association of Caribbean States are really necessary.

In the context of Caribbean unity the position of the Bahamas is a curious one.

The Bahamas have signaled a definite desire to participate in the Caribbean Community, but not the Common Market nor Single Economy. The other member states have indulged the Bahamas whose argument is that the structure of their economy and system of taxation militate against full participation in the regional movement.

There exists a very special regional subgrouping within Caricom known as The Organization of Eastern Caribbean States (O.E.C.S.).

This subgrouping demonstrates its own autonomy and even though each member of the subgrouping is also a full-fledged Caricom member OECS states appear to have more faith in their eastern Caribbean entity than the wider, broader organization.

There are functional agencies, associates of Caricom which need additional support and resources.

For example for years the University of the West Indies has been able to show that contributing member states have not been making (prompt) payments to the U.W.I.

The effect of this is to retard progress at the U.W.I.

The Caribbean Agricultural Research and Development Institute is another example of an associate of Caricom which has suffered from financial constraints occasioned by inadequate funding caused by non-payment of the subscriptions of member states.

A most important institution has been introduced to serve CARICOM and the CSME. This institution is the Caribbean Court of Justice (CCJ) which is located in Trinidad and Tobago. An interesting fact in respect of the CCJ is that although Caricom has no fewer than fifteen members only four states have so far been making use of its Appellate Court.

RESEARCH TASKS

1   Research the history of regional integration in the Caribbean.
2   Examine the biggest challenges to the ongoing success of regional integration
3   State three ways in which the work of the C.S.M.E. can advance the work of Caricom.
4   Research the work being done by the Caribbean institutions listed in this chapter.

QUESTIONS

1   Discuss the concepts of Tariffs, Excises, Exchange Control Orders, and Quotas
2   Comment on two objectives of the CSME
3   To what extent are the objectives of CARICOM being met?

CHAPTER 23

REGIONAL AND GLOBAL BUSINESS ENVIRONMENT

In this chapter there will be examination of a number of important institutions in which Caribbean territories may have an interest before considering some economic problems that face the Caribbean.

THE WORLD BANK

The World Bank exists to assist international territories to recover after problems such as the effect of hurricanes and other catastrophes have occurred. The World Bank also exists to provide funding for economies which cry out for development and growth. In addition it provides low interest loans and interest free credit and grants for the below:

(i)   education;
(ii)   health;
(iii)   infrastructure; and
(iv)   communications

The World Bank has put out an argument that it is committed to the reduction of poverty so much so that it seems to favour the poorest countries of the world. The World Bank is known to publish information on the reduction of poverty but of interest there are developing countries which are refused World Bank funding because the bank perceives them to be better off than poor. Some Caribbean countries have been disqualified from receiving World Bank assistance.

INTER-AMERICAN DEVELOPMENT BANK (IADB)

The IADB was set up in 1959 to assist in the financing of member countries and contribute to the acceleration of the process of economic and social development of regional developing member countries, individually and collectively.

(i)   the IADB applies its resources to the economies of Latin American and Caribbean countries;
(ii)   the IADB loans are advanced at rates of interest similar to those that are in existence in the borrowing countries. The IADB is empowered to provide financing out of its ordinary capital.
(iii)   The IADB has a fund for special operations resources;
(iv)   Some Caribbean countries have been able over the years to approach the IADB but the OECS many of whom are members of the OECS and the Association of Caribbean States do not access IADB funds.

ORGANISATION OF EASTERN CARIBBEAN STATES (OECS)

Founded on June 18, 1981 when seven Eastern Caribbean States signed a Treaty of Co-operation, the OECS currently has Antigua and Barbuda, Dominica, Grenada, Montserrat, St. Kitts/Nevis, St. Lucia and St. Vincent and the Grenadines as full members. Anguilla and British Virgin Islands feature as associate members of the OECS

The OECS operates as a sub-grouping within CARICOM and its mission is to be a major regional institution contributing to the sustainable development of the OECS member states by assisting them to maximize the benefits from their collective space, by facilitating the intelligent integration with the global economy, by contributing to policy and program formulation and execution in respect of regional and international issues and by the facilitation of bilateral and multilateral co-operation.

Aims of The OECS

To promote co-operation among member states:
  (i)   as far as possible to speak with one voice in regional and international affairs;
  (ii)   to promote unity and solidarity among member states;
  (iii)   to assist member states in meeting their international obligations;
  (iv)   to set out to harmonise their foreign policy in ways that would allow member states to take common positions on international issues;
  (v)   to promote economic integration among member states;
  (vi)   free movement of OECS citizens

ORGANISATION OF AMERICAN STATES (OAS)

The OAS was set up after the Second World War with the aims stated below:
  (i)   to strengthen the peace and security of the continents (North America, South America etc.;
  (ii)   to promote and consolidate representative democracy, with due respect for the principle of non-intervention;
  (iii)   to prevent possible causes of difficulties and to ensure the pacific settlement of disputes that may arise among the member states;
  (iv)   to provide for common action on the part of those states in the event of aggression;
  (v)   to seek the solution of political, judicial and economic problems that may arise among them;
  (vi)   to promote, by cooperative action, their economic, social and cultural development;
  (vii)   to eradicate extreme poverty, which constitutes an obstacle to the full democratic development of the peoples of the hemisphere;
  (viii) to achieve an effective limitation of conventional weapons that will make it possible to devote the largest amount of resources to the economic and social development of the member states.

ROLE AND PURPOSE OF ECONOMIC COMMISSION FOR LATIN AMERICA AND THE CARIBBEAN (ECLAC)

(i)   to provide important secretariat services and documents for the Commission and its member parts;

(ii)   to undertake studies, research and other support activities as far as the rules and resources of ECLAC would permit;

(iii) to promote economic and social development through regional and sub-regional operation and integration;

(iv)   to gather, organize, interpret and spread information which is relevant and relates to the economic and social development of Latin America and the Caribbean;

(v)   to provide advisory services to Governments in need of such;

(vi)   to plan and to assist in the planning and execution of programmes aimed at technical co-operation;

(vii) to organize conferences at the inter-governmental level and to sponsor training workshops, symposiums and seminars

WORLD TRADE ORGANISATION (WTO)

The World Trade Organisation is an institution that sees itself as having responsibility of liberalizing trade worldwide. It is therefore committed to the concept of free trade and in practice where countries offer subsidies to producers, allowing these producers to have unfair trading advantages, the WTO is opposed to that type of thing.

One of its primary goals is to encourage countries to negotiate their way towards legal trading agreements. It does not accept tariffs that it deems to be unfair and where some countries are allowed preferential treatment in respect of receiving favourable prices while competitors are not the beneficiaries of such preferences, the WTO opposes such practices.

Finally, where countries especially developing countries complain that they are not competing on level playing fields, the WTO is willing to allow for special and differential treatment to be granted to such countries.

CARIBBEAN BASIN INITIATIVE (CBI)

Coming into effect on 1st January, 1984 the general policy of the Caribbean Basin Initiative has been to provide a range of tax tariffs and trade benefits to Central American and Caribbean countries. The CBI is intended to facilitate the economic development and export diversification of Caribbean basin economies.

The CBI does actually provide duty free access to the US market for many goods coming from Antigua and Barbuda, Aruba, Bahamas, Barbados, Belize, British Virgin Islands, Costa Rica, Dominica, Dominican Republic, El Salvador, Grenada, Guatemala, Guyana, Haiti, Honduras,

Jamaica, Montserrat, Netherlands Antilles, Nicaragua, Panama, St. Kitts and Nevis, St. Lucia, St. Vincent and the Grenadines and Trinidad and Tobago.

ORGANIZATION OF PETROLEUM EXPORTING COUNTRIES (OPEC)

A grouping of oil producing countries including Venezuela but excluding Trinidad and Tobago is what the OPEC is.

In practice, OPEC is a cartel which combines the efforts of a number of oil producers to secure their interests especially by providing for policies on the pricing, export and control of their oil resources.

Where oil prices rise or are raised Caribbean governments and peoples will feel their effects so OPEC can never be ignored.

EASTERN CARIBBEAN COMMOM MARKET (ECCM)

Eastern Caribbean Common Market has grown out of the OECS and is the economic arm of the OECS. Since the ECCM is a common market the various countries that make up the OECS are brought together as one market where goods and services are freely traded.

CARIBBEAN CANADIAN AGREEMENT (CARIBCAN)

In January 2001, the Caricom and Canadian Heads of Government reached a decision in Jamaica to establish a joint working group to prepare a framework agreement on the scope and nature of a more mature trade and economic agreement to enhance existing arrangements and to culminate in a possible Free Trade Agreement. Since then some four meetings were held involving the CARICOM, Canada Joint Working Group and these meetings looked at the following areas:

(i)   the scope and content of negotiations;
(ii)   the exchange of information;
(iii) the question of market access for agriculture and industrial goods;

Other areas considered were investment, possible trading services and the settlement of disputes.

RESEARCH

1. Research the tangible contribution of the IADB to Caribbean countries. Provide examples.
2. Examine the positive and negative impacts of the WTO on Caribbean countries.
3. Study the influence of OPEC on oil-producing territories in the region.

QUESTIONS

1. Comment on the aims of the Organisation of Eastern Caribbean States.
2. Examine the role of the Organisation of American States and assess its relevance to Caribbean countries.

CHAPTER 24

ECONOMIC PROBLEMS IN THE CARIBBEAN

Many economic problems and challenges face Caribbean economies among which are:

1. Unemployment
2. Excessively High Populations
3. Emigration
4. High National Debt
5. Shortage of capital (Investment Funding)
6. Shortage of Technology
7. Economic Dualism
8. Inflation
9. HIV/AIDS

UNEMPLOYMENT

Unemployment can be defined as a situation where persons willing and able to work do not get opportunities to work and so earn no income.

SOME CAUSES OF UNEMPLOYMENT

1. Very High Populations.
2. Low level of qualifications and skills among job seekers.
3. Shortage of employment opportunities.
4. Seasonality of work opportunities in agriculture, tourism and other sectors.

CONSEQUENCES OF UNEMPLOYMENT

1. Poverty.
2. Frustration among those who cannot find work.
3. Crime.
4. A poor quality of life among the unemployed.
5. Dependence on the State for Welfare Services.

WAYS TO SOLVE UNEMPLOYMENT

1. Governments should seek to increase investment and job opportunities.
2. Governments should create more opportunities for education and training.
3. The population should be encouraged to increase its skills by (Multi-Skilling).
4. The activities of Family Planning Organizations should be strengthened.
5. Governments should encourage more self-employment.

EXCESSIVELY HIGH POPULATION

A population is excessively high where in a country there are too many mouths to feed.

CAUSES OF LARGE POPULATIONS

1. High rates of fertility are responsible for high populations.
2. Poor family planning practices are also a cause of high population.
3. An alarmingly high rate of teenage pregnancies contributes to high populations.

CONSEQUENCES OF HIGH POPULATIONS

1. Unemployment and underemployment.
2. Large informal sectors in the economies.
3. Poverty.
4. Lawlessness, drift and crime.
5. Some families are unable to feed and educate their infants.

SOLUTIONS TO THE PROBLEMS OF EXCESSIVE POPULATIONS

1. Improved family planning programmes.
2. Widespread public education programmes.
3. 'Special Care' programmes to assist many large families.
4. Emphasis on quality family life.
5. Programmes and education geared to reducing teenage pregnancies.

EMIGRATION

Emigration means movement of people out of the country.

CAUSES OF EMIGRATION

1. Not enough opportunities for locals in their home countries.
2. Locals fearing that they have no future in their own country.
3. A feeling by locals that overseas countries especially developed nations, offer more prospects than their own country.
4. Relatives abroad enticing their families and friends to migrate from their country of origin and residence.

CONSEQUENCES OF EMIGRATION

1. The local country loses significant numbers of their human resources.
2. In some cases there is a flight of capital.
3. The development of the 'sending country', i.e. the country which the emigrant leaves, is slowed down.

HOW TO TACKLE EMIGRATION

1. Government should try to have more industries established and working opportunities.
2. All citizens must be made to feel part of their country.
3. Ideas of patriotism and nationalism should be strengthened.
4. Employment opportunities should be increased.
5. To the extent that many emigrants migrate to study and to seek out training opportunities, Caribbean Governments should broaden the scope for local education and training.

HIGH NATIONAL DEBT

A Nation's debt may consist of locally raised borrowings together with loans raised from abroad.

CAUSES OF DEBT AT THE NATIONAL LEVEL

1. Insufficient money available to the nation.
2. Heavy local borrowing.
3. Money misspent or wasted meaning that much of the money available to Caribbean Governments is NOT put to proper use.
4. Relative shortage of Government revenue leading to Governments having to borrow.
5. The existence of large fiscal deficits.

CONSEQUENCES OF SIGNIFICANT LEVELS OF DEBT

1. Many projects never get going.
2. Governments increase taxes in the hope of capturing more revenue.
3. At the government level Government's expenditure constantly exceeds total Government revenue.
4. A kind of debt trap sets in where Government e.g. Guyana and Jamaica, have had to turn to the International Monetary Fund, the international lender of last resort.

The International Monetary Fund has caused countries, e.g. Guyana and Jamaica to devalue their currencies.

Devaluation has led to intolerable levels of inflation and poverty. Countries undertaking devaluations have also witnessed many of their able people in these territories emigrating.

HOW TO TACKLE HIGH DEBT

1. In most Caribbean countries there have been inadequate mechanisms to capture all the taxes due to Governments, the results being that in some territories while large amounts of taxes remain owing, Governments have still gone ahead and increased taxes.
2. Governments should clamp down on tax evasion.

3. High cost Government projects should be so managed so as to yield the best possible return.
4. Governments should identify areas of the wastage of public funds and seek to eliminate such wastage.

SHORTAGE OF CAPITAL

Where capital is defined as money which is invested in economic or commercial activity (investment finance) and a given country does not have enough funds for investment, a shortage of capital is in existence.

CAUSES OF CAPITAL SHORTAGE

1. Low levels of national savings.
2. Too many people see money solely as a means by which they can spend on consumer products.

Where Governments themselves are very short on money the levels of direct investment by Governments are low. Some Caribbean countries have proved to be unattractive to foreign investors who invest their money outside of the Caribbean.

CONSEQUENCES OF CAPITAL SHORTAGE

1. Relatively low level of investment.
2. Where investment is low, few new opportunities are created for employment.
3. Where there are low levels of investment on account of capital shortages, economic growth will be low or nonexistent.
4. Capital shortages can also mean that a country's development can be retarded.

TACKLING THE PROBLEM OF SHORTAGE OF INVESTMENT FUNDS

1. Government should offer special incentives to persuade their citizens to save.
2. Governments should participate in programmes by which seed capital should be made available to new businesses.
3. In areas where private sector business people do not invest, Government should make up for the shortfall.
4. A range of policies and programmes should be implemented to attract Foreign Direct Investment.

SHORTAGE OF TECHNOLOGY

Capital shortage can also mean, depending on the context, a shortage of machinery and equipment.

CAUSES OF THE SHORTAGE OF CAPITAL EQUIPMENT

1. The Caribbean region on a whole lacks the resources to produce its own machinery and equipment.
2. Over the years there has been insufficient research into indigenous Caribbean technologies.
3. Much of the modern equipment which can facilitate business and commercial activity is very costly.
4. There have been insufficient Government incentives geared to creating or importing new technologies.
5. The Caribbean region lacks the raw materials and factor inputs which can be used to introduce new technologies.

CONSEQUENCES OF THE SHORTAGE OF CAPITAL EQUIPMENT

1. Old fashioned methods are in existence.
2. Often labour has to be used in cases where developed countries make use of technology.
3. Production in the Caribbean is often quite costly.
4. Economies of scale are difficult to be achieved.
5. Large scale production on a mass production scale IS NOT achieved.

DEALING WITH SHORTAGES OF CAPITAL EQUIPMENT

1. Governments should offer incentives, fiscal and otherwise to encourage more Caribbean entrepreneurs to make use of technology.
2. Governments in the Caribbean should facilitate or create innovation programme and schemes.
3. Governments should encourage more indigenous investment in local research and development.
4. There should be serious intensive stock taking efforts to locate obsolete and outdated technologies.
5. The youth of the Caribbean should be encouraged to be innovative and enterprising with technology when they establish businesses.

ECONOMIC DUALISM

This can be defined as an economic situation where within the same country there is a marked difference between conditions in cities and towns on the one hand and rural districts on the other.

CAUSES OF ECONOMIC DUALISM

1. Much more investments in cities and towns than in rural areas.
2. More opportunities in cities and towns.

3. More modernity in cities and towns.

4. A greater and better level of infrastructure e.g. roads, electricity, piped water etc. in cities and towns than in rural areas.

5. Enterprising individuals abandoning rural areas and migrating to cities and towns.

CONSEQUENCES OF ECONOMIC DUALISM

1. The quality of life of persons in developed areas is superior to that of rural people.

2. Many rural areas especially in the larger Caribbean territories lack roads, schools, health care clinics and hospitals and even proper supplies of running water.

3. Many people rather than remain in rural areas 'run off' into cities and developed areas causing population pressure in the developed areas where some towns and cities are overcrowded with poor housing and slums coming into existence in many cities and towns.

4. Rural areas are at risk of de-population as people flee from them in search of opportunities in the developed lands.

5. Enterprises are in very small numbers in rural areas.

6. There is a disproportionate level of development favouring cities and towns while constraining progress in the rural areas.

POSSIBLE SOLUTIONS TO THE PROBLEM OF ECONOMIC DUALISM

1. Provide more roads, schools, bridges, better transport and such like in the rural areas.

2. Encourage investment in enterprises in the rural areas to:
    (a)   encourage the rural folks to remain in their district of origin; and
    (b)   to relieve population pressure in built-up areas, towns and cities.

3. Embark on sustainable programmes of rural development to
    (a)   develop rural enterprises;
    (b)   increase rural enterprises;
    (c)   allow rural areas to take a greater part in some of the development of the country.

4. Set deliberate policies by which things like investment, research and development and decent housing can be introduced into rural area.

5. Provide a range of economic incentives geared to attract and develop a stronger sense of enterprise and more businesses with the rural areas.

6. Since many rural areas have considerable amounts of space (Land), proper planning programmes designed to develop rural areas should be introduced.

INFLATION

Described as a persistent and sustained increase in the general level of prices inflation is caused by:

(a)   Shortages of a nature that make national aggregate demand exceed supply.

(b) A condition resulting from increase in the prices of raw materials and factor inputs, including labour.

(c) High levels of taxation on a wide range of goods and services.

(d) The importation of goods and services which are already costly in their countries of origin.

(e) Price gouging and excessive mark-ups which are associated with profiteering.

EFFECTS ON INFLATION

1. High Prices.
2. Decreases in the purchasing power of money.
3. Decreases in the standard of living especially of the poorer segments in the community.
4. Where inflation affects building materials, raw materials and factor inputs investments is slowed down and there could be decreases in the level of investment.
5. (a) Organized labour and trade unions feel compelled to demand large increases.
    (b) Many businesses that have to increase wages pass the increases
    to consumers in inflation.
6. When inflation is very bad it is called runaway inflation or galloping inflation. There is also the concept of stagflation.

TACKLING THE PROBLEMS OF INFLATION

Government should do the following:

1. Establish departments specially set up to deal with price gouging.
2. Rather than rely heavily on imports attempt to produce more local goods especially food items.
3. Reduce burdensome taxes.
4. Embark on or buy local companies.
5. (a) Manage the national economies well enough to avoid having to borrow from the International Monetary Fund.
    (b) The International Monetary Fund (IMF) has by insisting on devaluation especially in Guyana and Jamaica caused the currency of these two nations to decrease in value with the result of higher prices for almost all commodities.
6. Increase productivity in the country.
7. Be selective in how the local Caribbean countries 'shop around' for goods and services.

HIV/AIDS

Initially the problem of HIV/AIDS was perceived as a medical problem. However since this matter bears potential to kill and reduce productive members of our community HIV/AIDS definitely has a human resource dimension to it.

CAUSES

- Infection by blood from needles used by drug addicts.
- To some extent sexual promiscuity.
- Without being promiscuous infection by a partner who might not have known that they were carriers of HIV.
- Up to a limited extent blood transfusions. This was so in the early days but nowadays there is proper testing.

CONSEQUENCES

- Early death.
- Rapid decline in health preceding death.
- Further spread of the virus, often innocently.
- Threats to destroy our human resources especially our youth.
- High cost of treating victims.
- Babies born to affected mothers are orphaned.
- Where HIV/AIDS is widespread by causing early death among our people, productive human resource are under threat and our region's forward development can be compromised.
- HIV/AIDS is a threat to our human resources.

POSSIBLE SOLUTIONS

1. The practice of safe sex by means of sticking to one faithful partner.
2. Widespread use of condoms.
3. Massive public education and sensitization.

There are other economic problems which face the Caribbean some of which are linked to particular social problems.

The problems discussed here tend to be the major ones in the Caribbean countries and are economic in nature. There are other social problems in the Caribbean which readers should research.

RESEARCH TASKS

1. How can crime affect economic activity?
2. List the incentives which Caribbean Governments have offered foreign investors.
3. What measures or strategies ought Caribbean Governments to use to deal with inflation?
4. How can a country control its National Debt?
5. Do you agree that large populations can present economic problems?
6. Research the concept of stagflation
7. Research Governments' offer of special incentives to local businesses.

QUESTIONS

1. Explain four causes of emigration.
2. Comment on the impact of emigration.
3. Describe inflation and examine the impact of inflation on two Caribbean countries.
4. Explain the impact of high debt on two Caribbean countries.
5. Comment on the consequences of devaluation using two Caribbean countries as examples.

MULTIPLE CHOICE QUESTIONS

SELECT THE BEST ANSWER(S) IN EACH OF THE BELOW

1. Which of these is not a basic need for human survival?
    (a)   Food.
    (b)   Jewelry.
    (c)   Clothes.
    (d)   Shelter.

        (i) a only   (ii) b only   (iii) c only   (iv) d only

2. With barter:
    (a)   Finding the correct trading partner is difficult.
    (b)   It is easy to know the availability of goods.
    (c)   Economies characterized by barter offer services in huge quantities.
    (d)   Barter is the main characteristic of centrally planned economies.

        (i) a only   (ii) b only   (iii) c only   (iv) d only

3. The use of money in trade:-
    (a)   Makes bartering arrangements easier.
    (b)   Encourages persons to credit.
    (c)   Serves as a means of exchange.
    (d)   Restricts the quantities of goods which may be traded.

        (i) a only   (ii) b only   (iii) c only   (iv) d only

4. Which of these is NOT an example of primary production?
    (a)   The manufacture and production of lap-top computers.
    (b)   The mining of bauxite.
    (c)   The sale of rooms in a condominium complex.
    (d)   The canning of tomatoes.

        (i)a only   (ii) a, b and c   (iii)a and c   (iv)a, c and d

5. Secondary Production is:
    (a)   A stage higher than primary production.
    (b)   The management of offshore banks.
    (c)   The construction of middle-income houses.
    (d)   The organized systematic method of netting and catching fish.

        (i) a only   (ii)a and c   (iii)b only   (iv)c and d

6.   'Utility' means:
   (a)   The general use to which goods are put.
   (b)   A kind of usefulness.
   (c)   The satisfaction people derive from their consumption of goods and services.
   (d)   Another word for productivity.

        (i)a only   (ii)b only   (iii)c only   (iv) d only

7.   Perishable goods last longer and are more useful:
   (a)   When they are traded within a month or two.
   (b)   They are processed at the secondary stage of production.
   (c)   When they would have been properly manicured during their growth.
   (d)   When by means of impulse buying they are bought at the same time as non-perishable goods.

        (i) a only   (ii) b only   (iii) c only   (iv) d only

.8   Economics can be defined as:
   (a)   That branch of science which focuses entirely/directly on people's health.
   (b)   An area of study which brings about unity in a nation.
   (c)   A behavioural science that encourages people to do good deeds.
   (d)   The study of the allocation of scarce resources.

        (i) a only   (ii) a and b   (iii) d only   (iv) b and d

9   A free enterprise economy is one in which:-
   (a)   Private individuals and firms are allowed to develop and manage their enterprises with but little government control.
   (b)   Citizens have unlimited freedoms.
   (c)   The government does not micro-manage individual firms and enterprises.
   (d)   Subject to taxation, laws and specific rules investors operating in the country are allowed to keep and share in any profits which are made.

        (i) a, c and d   (ii) b only   (iii) b and c   (iv) a and b

10   A centrally planned economy is one in which:-
   (a)   Private individuals are provided with incentives and finance to invest for profit.
   (b)   Government controls the factors of production and the commanding heights of the economy.
   (c)   There is little or no investment by private individuals.
   (d)   There is substantial free enterprise activity.

        (i) d only   (ii) c and d   (iii) a and d   (iv) b and c only

11   The term 'resources' refers to:-
       (a)   Consumer goods.
       (b)   Consumer services.
       (c)   Various economic items and amenities available for exploration in the
               country.
       (d)   Highly skilled workers whose productivity is high.

               (i) c only   (ii) a and c   (iii) a only

12   The best definition of an entrepreneur is
       (a)   A Manager.
       (b)   The Chief Executive Officer.
       (c)   An enterprising person who launches a business.
       (d)   The supplier of working capital for a business.

               (i) a only   (ii) a and b   (iii) c only   (iv) a and d

13   Examples of working capital are:-
       (a)   Money to meet the cost of utilities.
       (b)   Money invested in office equipment.
       (c)   Money spent on land.
       (d)   Money spent on buildings.

               (i) a only   (ii) a and b   (iii) a, b and c   (iv) all of the above.

14   The term 'capital' can mean:-
       (a)   All of the money a business handles.
       (b)   Money which is invested in machinery.
       (c)   The income made by a business.
       (d)   Money invested in plant and equipment.

               (i) a and c   (ii) b and d   (iii) b only   (iv) c only

15   The best definition of fixed capital is:-
       (a)   All the costs necessary to keep a business alive.
       (b)   The money provided by investors in a business.
       (c)   Investment in long-term assets such as plant and equipment.
       (d)   The costs of utilities and rent.

               (i) a only`   (ii) b only (iii) c only (iv) all of the above

16   Surplus production always refers to:
(a)   Trading by means of barter.
(b)   Producing goods by means of the latest technology.
(c)   Specialization and the division of labour.
(d)   The production of goods in such quantities that production exceeds the wants of the producer.

        (i) a only   (ii) b only   (iii) c only   (iv) d only

17.   The best definition of net profit is:
(a)   All money made after the sale of goods and services.
(b)   That money which is left after all expenses are deducted.
(c)   Income that does not disregard utilities, wages and advertising.
(d)   All of the items recorded in the capital and liabilities column of the business.

        (i) a only   (ii) b only   (iii) a and b   (iv) d only

18   A business which records a gross profit may still end up making a loss after:
(a)   Deducting its debt from the value of its total sales.
(b)   The cost of sales is lower than the value of sales.
(c)   Its accounts receivable from its debtors are being paid in at irregular intervals.
(d)   In addition to the cost of sales deductions are made from current expenses such as wages, utilities etc.

        (i) a only   (ii) b only   (iii) c only   (iv) d only

19   A business in the private sector is usually established to make and achieve profit but in practice other important purposes exist such as:-
(a)   To promote local sports.
(b)   To employ workers.
(c)   To support the Government.
(d)   To support local culture.

        (i) a only   (ii) b only   (iii) c only   (iv) d only

20.   A sole trader :-
(a)   Is free to open and close as he/her wishes.
(b)   Offers personalized service.
(c)   Can decide which customers are worthy of credit.
(d)   Keeps all profits made in his/her business.

        (i) a only   (ii) a and b   (iii) a, b and c   (iv) all of the above.

21.   The advantages partnerships enjoy are:-
       (a)   More capital becomes available.
       (b)   Partners are known to overwork by not getting proper help from
              their associates.
       (c)   Partners can share information.
       (d)   Individual partners may bring special skills to the firm.

              (i) a only   (ii) a and c   (iii) c and d   (iv) a, c and d

22.   The normal everyday partnership is:-
       (a)   Both a Firm and a Company.
       (b)   Bears unlimited liability.
       (c)   Has limited liability status.
       (d)   Is a firm but not a company.

              (i) a only   (ii) b and d   (iii) a and c   (iv) d only

23.   A multinational business is one which is likely:-
       (a)   To bring in all of its workers from many different nations.
       (b)   To be incorporated.
       (c)   To access the latest technological equipment.
       (d)   To establish branches of its business in several countries.

              (i) a only   (ii) b only   (iii) c only   (iv) b, c and d

24   Among the challenges faced by small enterprises are –
       (a)   Shortages of capital.
       (b)   Hostility by financiers.
       (c)   Oppressive regulations by governments.
       (d)   Competition from larger business units.

              (i) a and c   (ii) a and b   (iii) a and d   (iv) a, b and d

25   The span of management or span of control refers to:
       (a)   The numbers of employees who work under management.
       (b)   A grouping of employees down the scale who come together
              under a shop steward.
       (c)   A system of internal organization designed to bring about
              effective supervision.
       (d)   A system of workers' committees who answer to their trade
              union.

              (i) a only   (ii) a and c   (iii) b only   (iv) b and d

26.   In cases where the chain of command exists as a Pyramid:-
      (a)   Layers of power and authority are clearly set out.
      (b)   Those at the top of the pyramid wield the most power and authority.
      (c)   Those who occupy the lower rungs are frequently consulted on major issues and decisions.
      (d)   The pyramid is established as a means of convenience.

      (i) a only   (ii) a and b   (iii) a and c   (iv) d only

27.   Under the system of functional organization the firm is characterized by:-
      (a)   A narrow pyramid.
      (b)   The division of the business entity into specific departments, each with its own manager.
      (c)   The Manager or Chief Executive Officer makes all of the decisions.
      (d)   There are strong effective workers' committees.

      (i) a only   (ii) b only   (iii) c only   (iv) d only

28.   Under the line and staff organization:-
      (a)   Lines of authority are kept clear.
      (b)   The line organization is combined with the functional organisation.
      (c)   The structure known as the pyramid is brought into existence.
      (d)   The directors of the firm frequently instruct managers and supervisors at all levels of the firm.

      (i) a and c   (ii) c and d   (iii) a only   (iv) a and b

29   An authoritarian leader is likely to:-
      (a)   Keep supervision down to a minimum.
      (b)   Take decisions without consulting the broad masses of workers.
      (c)   Fail or refuse to delegate.
      (d)   Keep frequent meetings and consultations with staff.

      (i) a only   (ii) b only   (iii)b and c   (iv) a, b and c

30   One of the obvious weaknesses of the democratic style of leadership is:-
      (a)   It provides opportunities for all types of feedback.
      (b)   It can be slow and hesitant.
      (c)   It is too autocratic.
      (d)   It places no emphasis on supervision.

      (i) a only   (ii) b only   (iii) c only   (iv) d only

31.   An example of secondary research is:-

(a)   The results of a very specially prepared questionnaire.

(b)   Government records and statistics covering the past ten years.

(c)   Information in a magazine published by the Chamber of Commerce.

(d)   General information in a popular consumer magazine.

(i) a only   (ii) a and d   (iii) a and c   (iv) b, c and d

32.   Generic advertising is:-

(a)   The advertising of a branded new product.

(b)   Promoting a commodity by use of attractive labels.

(c)   Advertising geared to defeat any competition in the market place.

(d)   Information on a particular good or commodity of a general nature which is non-persuasive.

(i) a only   (ii) b only   (iii) c only   (iv) d only

33.   Persuasive advertising would probably:-

(a)   Present products in a simple manner.

(b)   Make exaggerated claims about product quality.

(c)   Merely present factual information.

(d)   Be labeled and packaged in highly attractive ways.

(i)a and c   (ii) b only   (iii) b and d   (iv) d only

34   The basic chain of distribution which has no modifications consists of

(a)   Two links.

(b)   Five links.

(c)   Four links.

(d)   Three links.

(i) a only   (ii) b only   (iii) c only   (iv) d only

35.   When goods are imported, one result is:-

(a)   An outflow of foreign exchange.

(b)   An inflow of foreign exchange.

(c)   Occasions where the imports enter the Caribbean under special arrangements.

(d)   More goods and wider choices become available to the local market.

(i) b and c   (ii) a and c   (iii) a and d   (v) d only

36.   Which of these is NOT a feature of Perfect Competition?
        (a)   No single buyer can fix the final price.
        (b)   No single seller can set the market price.
        (c)   There are but few buyers and sellers.
        (d)   Businesses can enter and leave the market as they please.

                (i) a only   (ii) a and c   (iii) c only   (iv) b and d only

37   An open economy is best described as one in which:-
        (a)   The economy is able to produce all of the market's needs.
        (b)   There are many producers producing above basic subsistence.
        (c)   The economy's exports exceed its imports.
        (d)   The economy's imports exceed its exports.

                (i) a only   (ii) a and b   (iii) b and c   (iv) d only

38.   A monopoly exists where:-
        (a)   There is open competition among a variety of suppliers.
        (b)   One firm controls the production of goods and services.
        (c)   There are a few producers only.
        (d)   There is but one buyer.

                (i) a only   (ii) b only   (iii) c only   (iv) c and d

39   A well-known trademark can:-
        (a)   Beat off competition.
        (b)   Generate goodwill among the buying public.
        (c)   Increase sales.
        (d)   Make no difference as to how a product performs on the market.

                (i) a and b   (ii) b and c   (iii) a, b and c   (iv) d only

40   A franchise is:-
        (a)   A legal arrangement by which a third party is given authority to sell and trade in the product of the owner of the product.
        (b)   A mere agency contract.
        (c)   A system of sales by which commissions are paid to the owner of a patent.
        (d)   The protection given to a seller to prevent them from encountering unfair competition.

                (i) a only   (ii) b only   (iii) c only   (iv) d only

41   The purpose of a patent is to:-
        (a)   Advertise a product.
        (b)   Protect the rights of an inventor of a product.
        (c)   Trademark a product.
        (d)   Allow a product to be sold with complementary goods.

        (i) a only   (ii) a and c   (iii) b only   (iv) d only

42   The government department where patents and trademarks are recorded is said to `
        be:-
        (a)   A Commercial Government Department.
        (b)   A type of clearing house.
        (c)   A branch of the High Court.
        (d)   The Regulator of Intellectual Property.

        (i) a only   (ii) b only   (iii) c only   (iv) d only

43.   In the market place a substitute is:-
        (a)   Another product that a consumer can use as a close second choice.
        (b)   A complementary good or service.
        (c)   A product in demand only during particular seasons.
        (d)   An affordable product or service.

        (i) a only   (ii) b only   (iii) c only   (iv) d only

44.   Which of the below are complementary goods:-
        (a)   Ackee and Saltfish.
        (b)   Rum and Coke.
        (c)   Sprite and Soda (Club Soda).
        (d)   Cheese and Corn.

        (i) a and b   (ii) b and c   (iii) c and d   (iv) a, b, c and d

45   Consumers need protection because:-
        (a)   They are not always able to bargain effectively with suppliers.
        (b)   Everyone needs protection.
        (c)   Some suppliers and providers like to do as they please.
        (d)   Experience has shown that some consumers have fallen victim to unfair
                practices.

        (i) a only.   (ii) b only.   (iii) a, c and d   (iv) d only.

46   Under the law goods and services must:-
(a)   Be sold as cheaply as possible.
(b)   Conform with how they were advertised.
(c)   Be indigenously produced and not brought in from overseas.
(d)   Be sold to the highest bidder.

(i) a only.   (ii) b only.   (iii) a and c   (iv) d only.

47.   Two examples of what Government does to protect consumers are:-
(a)   Make Rules that govern the sale of food.
(b)   Fund private bodies for the purpose of providing assistance.
(c)   Set Price controls on select items.
(d)   Invite consumers to contribute to a central fund for purposes of subsidizing products and services.

(i) a and c   (ii) a and b   (iii) b and d   (iv) c only.

48.   Indicate which of the below statements is true:-
(a)   Caricom takes an interest in the standards and quality of goods.
(b)   Caricom is disinterested in what happens in the market especially where market forces are concerned.
(c)   Within recent times the cost of living has attracted the attention of Caricom.
(d)   It is for the Commonwealth Secretariat to deal with consumer issues within Caricom.

(i) a and d   (ii) b and d   (iii) a and d   (iv) a and c

49   Overdrafts are connected to:-
(a)   Current and Chequeing Accounts.
(b)   Credit Transfers.
(c)   Standing Orders.
(d)   Fixed Deposits.

(i) a only   (ii) b only   (iii) c only   (iv) d only

50.   Where a client is allowed overdraft facilities, he/ she can:-
(a)   Access managers' drafts at will.
(b)   Write cheques for more money than what is on his/her current or chequeing account.
(c)   Avoid bank charges on their current or chequeing account.
(d)   Avoid stamp duty.

(i) a only   (ii) b only   (iii) c only   (i) d only

51.   When making payments through the mail and postal system it is best to send:-
(a)   Cash.
(b)   An open cheque.
(c)   A bearer cheque.
(d)   A bank draft.

(i) a only   (ii) b only   (iii) c only   (v) d only

52   Which of these is NOT a function of a Central Bank?
(a)   To offer loans and advances to the public at large.
(b)   To provide Banking Services to the Government.
(c)   To provide Banking Services to Commercial Banks.
(d)   To issue all coins and currency of the country.

(i) a only   (ii) b only   (iii) c only   (iv) d only

53   Endorsing a cheque means:
(a)   Presenting it to a commercial bank.
(b)   Signing its back as payee .
(c)   Lodging the cheque with one's bank for five or six days.
(d)   Depositing it to one's account.

(i) a only   (ii) b only   (iii) c only   (iv) d only

54.   Credit Unions are:-
(a)   Financial Co-operatives.
(b)   Building Societies.
(c)   Co-operative Commercial Banking Institutions.
(d)   Informal savings societies.

(i) a only   (ii) b only   (iii) c only   (iv) d only

55   An actuary is –
(a)   A principal advisor of the company for which he works.
b)   One who sells policies of insurance.
(c)   A specialist statistician.
d)   A broker.

(i) b and d   (ii) a and c   (iii) a and d   (iv) d only.

56   The best description of a person who sells and arranges life insurance coverage for the public at large is:-

(a)   A broker.

(b)   A Life Underwriter.

(c)   An assessor.

(d)   An actuary.

(i) a and b   (ii) b only   (iii) c and d   (iv) a and d only.

57.   Provide the best answer from the following:

(a)   Every contract must be written up.

(b)   Contracts under seal still require consideration.

(c)   Every contract manifests an intention to create legal relations.

(d)   A contract is a legally enforceable arrangement.

(i) c only   (ii) a and c   (iii) c and d   (iv) a and d

58   Select the best answer from this question.

A contract is terminated in an acceptable manner when:

(a)   By mutual agreement backed by accord and satisfaction when the parties to the contract agree not to proceed with the original contract.

(b)   The parties to the 'deal' all perform their obligations under the contract.

(c)   An unforeseeable supervening event disrupts the performance of the 'deal'.

(d)   A fourteen year old minor refuses to pay $800,000 for a mini mansion.

(i) a and d.   (ii) a only   (iii) a, b and c.   (iv) b and d.

59.   It can be said that English-speaking Caribbean governments supervise:-

(a)   Collectivist Systems.

(b)   Centrally Planned Systems.

(c)   Command Economic Systems.

(d)   Mixed Economic Systems.

(i) a only   (ii) b and c   (iii) d only   (iv) none of the above

60.   Inflation can best be described as -

(a)   Marked increases in the general level of prices.

(b)   Moderate increases in the cost of capital goods.

(c)   An increase of 5% in the prices of food.

(d)   Increases in the cost of bank overdrafts.

(i)   b only   (ii) a only   (iii) b and c   (iv) c only

ANSWERS TO MULTIPLE CHOICE QUESTIONS

1	2	3	4	5	6	7	8	9	10	11	12
(i)	(i)	(iii)	(iv)	(ii)	(iii)	(ii)	(iii)	(i)	(iv)	(i)	(iii)

13	14	15	16	17	18	19	20	21	22	23	24
(i)	(ii)	(iii)	(iv)	(ii)	(iv)	(ii)	(iv)	(iv)	(ii)	(iv)	(iii)

25	26	27	28	29	30	31	32	33	34	35	36
(ii)	(ii)	(ii)	(iv)	(ii)	(ii)	(iv)	(iv)	(iii)	(iv)	(iii)	(iv)

37	38	39	40	41	42	43	44	45	46	47	48
(iv)	(ii)	(iii)	(i)	(iii)	(iv)	(i)	(i)	(iii)	(ii)	(i)	(iv)

49	50	51	52	53	54	55	56	57	58	59	60
(i)	(ii)	(iv)	(i)	(ii)	(i)	(ii)	(ii)	(iii)	(iii)	(iii)	(ii)

ABOUT THE AUTHORS

RAWLE CYPRIAN EASTMOND

Rawle Cyprian Eastmond received his secondary education at the Coleridge & Parry School, Barbados before proceeding to the Barbados Community College and the University of the West Indies where he completed a BA (General) with honours specializing in Economics, History and Politics. On graduation he pursued a career in teaching at the secondary school level and completed his Diploma in Education. He taught Principles of Business for CSEC Examinations of the Caribbean Examinations Council and was an Assistant Examiner for the subject at the CSEC (CXC) Exams for over ten years.

Mr.Eastmond undertook studies in Law with the University of London, graduating with an LLB (Hons). After furthering his studies in Law at the Hugh Wooding Law School in Trinidad & Tobago and completing his Legal Education Certificate he took up law practice in Barbados. He later pursued post-graduate studies in Law and was awarded the LLM. (Leicester University). He also completed a Certificate in Business with the Heriot -Watt University.

Mr. Eastmond was Member of Parliament in the Barbados House of Assembly from 1991 and served undefeated until 2008. He was a Minister from 1994 until 2008. He held the portfolios of Agriculture and Rural Development; Environment, Energy and Natural Resources; and Labour and Social Security at various times during his tenure.

Mr . Eastmond is the author of five other books namely 'Yardfowl', 'Helen's Hound', 'Unshackled', 'Beach Bum' and 'Woman'.

WENDELL CHARLES CHRISTOPHER CALLENDER

Wendell Charles Christopher Callender attended Harrison College, Barbados and furthered his education at the University of the West Indies where he completed the BA (General) majoring in Economics ; the Diploma in Education; and BSc (Hons) in Public Administration. He also completed studies leading to the award of Certificates in Marketing and Law (BIMAP)

Mr. Callender served as a teacher and administrator at the secondary school level for over twenty years. He also tutored at post –secondary level at the Caribbean Training Institute and the School of Continuing Studies of the University of the West Indies. He taught Principles of Business to the CSEC level of the Caribbean Examinations Council and Business Studies Advanced Level for University of Cambridge International Examinations. Mr. Callender also conducted training seminars in Selling, Customer service and Supervisory Management throughout the Caribbean and has worked as a Marketing Consultant to the Caribbean Confederation of Credit Unions.

Mr. Callender's other work experience includes being a Supervisor at the Central Bank of Barbados, Marketing Officer at the Barbados Tourism Authority, Executive Director of the Barbados Manufacturers' Association, Principal of Caribbean Training Institute and Executive Director of Marketing Specialists (C'bean) Ltd. He has also served as a Director on the Barbados Chamber of Commerce and Industry, President of the Barbados Association of Public Relations Practitioners and General Secretary of the Caribbean Association of Industry & Commerce.

Mr. Callender was a Member of Parliament and Chairman of Committees of the Barbados House of Assembly. He was a Chairman of the Barbados Agricultural Development and Marketing Corporation. This author was also a Shadow Minister of Education, Culture, Youth Affairs, Community Development and Sports.

Mr. Callender has worked as a columnist with the Nation Publishing Co. Ltd, has produced and presented radio programmes and has hosted radio talk shows. He is the author of four books entitled ' Prime Ministers of Barbados', 'Tools for Life-A practical guide for personal development', 'Many Sides of Barbados', and 'Handbook on Leadership'.

www.ingramcontent.com/pod-product-compliance
Lightning Source LLC
Chambersburg PA
CBHW080637180526
45168CB00008B/3208